Harold's STORY

A Journey of
Uncommon
Healing

Dr. Sam Mayhugh
with
D. Paul Thomas

Trilogy Christian Publishers
A Wholly Owned Subsidiary of Trinity Broadcasting Network
2442 Michelle Drive
Tustin, CA 92780

For information, address Trilogy Christian Publishing
Rights Department, 2442 Michelle Drive, Tustin, Ca 92780.
Trilogy Christian Publishing/ TBN and colophon are trademarks of Trinity Broadcasting Network.

For information about special discounts for bulk purchases, please contact Trilogy Christian Publishing.

10 9 8 7 6 5 4 3 2 1

Library of Congress Cataloging-in-Publication Data is available.

ISBN 978-1-64088-513-4 (Print Book)
ISBN 978-1-64088-514-1 (ebook)

In memory of

Gary Bayer and Pastor Earl Lee

Acknowledgments

This book was first conceived over forty years ago. A special thanks to a few individuals along the way who have contributed to its completion is apt.

First, thanks to the Reverend Paul Moore Jr. for his bold vision in starting Lamb's Ministries in the heart of Times Square.

Thanks also to my wife Arlene, Ms. Rinndy LeMaster, and Terri Mayhugh for transcribing Harold's audio tapes into five hundred pages of copy, capturing Harold's idioms and unique style in the process.

A thank-you to Shelley Thomas, whose photos of Harold's old haunts grace these pages.

Thanks to Dr. Earl Lee, former pastor of First Church of the Nazarene, Pasadena, California, whose friendship has been beyond measure. My Bible is filled with years of notes from his sermons.

Thanks to Gary Bayer, actor and storyteller extraordinaire, and his equally talented wife, Cindy, whose encouragement and advice in writing Harold's story have been invaluable. Conversations with them at their "place of stories" in Israel kept Harold's story in the foreground of my mind. Gary recently passed away after a long battle with cancer. Along with other saints, he rests in peace on Mt. Zion in Jerusalem.

And a big thanks to author Bob Goff, for referring me to Ms. Ally Fallon. Ally helps writers design and structure a "book in a day." Our full day of her "author coaching" was the catalyst for the year of joyful work which followed.

Also, thanks to D. Paul Thomas—a dear friend, actor, essayist, playwright and producer—whose initial editing resulted in my request that he assist in the writing and final design of the book.

Most of all, thanks to Harold for courageously sharing his story with us and for trusting me to help tell it!

Contents

Introduction

It was 1974. Other than the impending turbulence of Watergate, it was a relatively peaceful time. The Paris Peace Accords had been signed, and the Vietnam War was winding down. I was living a tranquil life with my wonderful wife, Arlene, and our two sons, Brian and Todd. I was a clinical psychologist with a comfortable private practice in Southern California, serving on the board of a growing church in Pasadena. Little did I know then that my comfortable life was about to be radically altered.

One Sunday, a small group of young people from the "Jesus Movement" in New Jersey came and participated in our service. Led by the dynamic Reverend Paul Moore Jr., they shared an audacious dream—a dream to purchase an old building in the heart of Times Square to serve the homeless and artistic communities (frequently, one and the same!) and liberate young woman from the burgeoning sex trafficking industry of New York City. Oh, and there was to be a church anchoring this creative ministry which would welcome *everyone* without judgment or exception! They called their mission the "Manhattan Project."

Their spirit and enthusiasm for a holistic, multifaceted Christian ministry in the inner city captured my imagination. Their proposal was direct: the historic Lamb's Club at 130 West 44th Street in Manhattan was for sale and all these young visionaries needed was $30,000 to initiate the project.

At a Sunday evening service, the congregation decided to take on the "Manhattan Project" as a missionary endeavor and donate the entire $30,000! Coincidentally, our church had been saving funds to support the next phase of its *own* property development. Even so, the board met immediately after the service and, following some spirited conversation, voted to contribute an additional $10,000 from its own expansion fund toward the purchase of the iconic Lamb's Club, the oldest professional theatrical club in America.

It was obvious that much work was still needed to be done to make this audacious dream a reality. Dick Birkey (a good friend and fellow parishioner from Pasadena) and I decided to visit the new Lamb's Ministries and offer our services. Dick was a talented commercial artist and would assist in the graphic development of an attractive logo and other vitally needed printed materials. By God's grace, I accepted the daunting assignment of developing a professional counseling clinic in the facility and to recruit and train counselors and coaches to work with the homeless, the abused women, and other individuals who needed special support.

Over the next two years, commuting from Los Angeles to New York several days a week, my life and practice would be transformed—meeting with actors, writers, musicians, the marginalized, abused and exploited—all whose stories and friendships challenged everything I thought I knew about healing and love. For it was here, at "the Lamb's," that I met Harold. This is *his* story—Harold's story—a journey of uncommon healing.

Early publicity photo
for the Lamb's Church

Prologue

By 1976, Harold was living in one of the smaller rooms located on the sixth floor of the Lamb's Ministries that provided shelter for homeless men and other individuals requiring special care. The fifth floor was exclusively for women. These two floors had once housed famous and not-so-famous actors, but none were more colorful than Harold. Though high-strung with a high-pitched voice to match, one's first impression of Harold was that of a rugged boxer—muscular, tightly wound, and ready to pounce if sufficiently provoked.

Our first chance meeting was on a bus ride with the Lamb's staff to a Sunday-night African American church service in Brooklyn. Harold chatted with me briefly on the bus and then cautiously asked if he could sit with me during the service, which turned out to be a rather spirited one for this laid-back Southern California psychologist. As the gospel choir reached a fervent pitch, emotions could not be contained. The congregants clapped and raised their hands heavenward, repeating over and over, "Thank you, Jesus! Thank you, Jesus!" in a joyful mantra of praise. Their enthusiasm was contagious, and Harold and I were soon joining in!

From that day on, we often sat together in the services at "the Lamb's," as it was popularly called. Although he never requested therapy, Harold would frequently make his way down to the counseling center on the fourth floor and ask me questions about psychology and life in general. An authentic friendship was developing as he slowly began sharing with me the more personal details of his life.

His memory was phenomenal, easily going all the way back to when he was four years old, vividly recalling periods of anxiety, depression, and anger. Somehow, Harold had survived a life of emotional, physical, and sexual abuse—a life of crime, prison, and psychiatric hospitals, accompanied by a broken marriage. How was it, I wondered, that Harold was now able to function at a relatively high level and be a positive influence among his contemporaries at the Lamb's, especially those experiencing painful and destructive life issues? Increasingly, I began to realize that Harold's life represented a multifaceted caricature, reflecting many aspects of the patients whom I had treated in private practice. Perhaps Harold's story held a key, or numerous keys, to the healing process?

Prompted by these questions, I suggested to Harold that his life story might benefit others in need of healing. Having only the equivalent of a sixth-grade education, Harold asked if I would help him tell his story. I told him that I would, but that it would have to be *his* story, spoken in *his* words. I soon provided him with a tape recorder and a box of blank tapes. I gave him weekly assignments, encouraging him to recall the details of distant memories. Little did I know then that my encouragement would result in Harold dictating over five hundred pages of a tortuous life journey—a life that begins with abandonment and abuse.

Old Lambs Flag

Chapter 1

The Attic

Cruelty kills the human spirit.

DR. SAM: I was privately ensconced in my Pasadena office and had told my secretary to hold the calls. Harold had sent me the first tape. With a sense of anticipation, I hit the Start button on the cassette recorder, wondering what his first words would be. As all good storytellers do, Harold began at the beginning.

HAROLD: I was four years old, and my earliest memory is I'm on this lawn, I'm at this home, and I'm with my brother, Theodore. I think he was sent there the same day or the day before, but anyway, I remember me and Theodore being at this home on the front lawn of a cottage, and there was this matron of the home [orphanage]. Her name was Miss Banderhoff, and there were some other kids there, and I was bawling, and I was cold, and I was… I was really petrified—so scared—just a scared little boy. I tell ya, Dr. Sam, I just felt so forlorn.

I was so scared of Miss Banderhoff. I don't know. I just felt that she was overpowering in some kind of cruel way. It frightened me because she always said that

I was her pet. She even changed my name—she called me Riley. She didn't call me by my real name, Harold. I was hurt and angry that she changed my name. She said, "We're going to call you, Riley." Who was she to take away my name? Who was she to be my keeper? She had no right over my life. I felt, why do I have to be here, why do I have to have this person be my mother? She said, "I like you better than my son, and I want to call you Riley." Well, she took my name away, called me Riley, and I hated her for it.

DR. SAM: At a very early age, the seeds of hatred were planted in Harold's psyche. Whether by design or default, Miss Banderhoff was setting the stage for Harold to experience a life of isolation and fear.

HAROLD: I was like the youngest kid there, and I don't know if it was right away or not, but after a while, when we would eat in the dining room, there was this big staff table at one end, and just when I started to feel at home with the kids, starting to get used to it, she separated me from all the other boys and made me sit at the staff table. She put a white napkin around me and put me on two boxes—not telephone books—but like two Sears and Roebuck catalogs that she'd put on this little chair they had put there. I was the only kid that sat with staff. She sat me there so prim and proud, and I felt so ashamed, like, you know, I felt I don't know these people, I don't know who they are, and she treats me like some kind of prize, a prize possession of hers, and she was going to make me, train me, make me be proper, and eat with the right spoon and all that stuff and make me the example.

I was just a little boy, and I didn't know what was happening. They'd all sit at the staff table and they'd say prayers and be together, all these adults, and I was the only little kid among them all. I was frightened of them and I didn't like them, but I couldn't say anything. I was being posed by her for everyone to see. And I'd look back there at the dining room, I'd look at all my friends there—well, they weren't really my friends yet—but they were strangers too, and I felt they hated me because I was getting special attention. I felt I wasn't part of them. I just felt so alone and scarred.

DR. SAM: By isolating him from the other boys, Harold became an object of their attention and eventual ridicule. Fortunately, there were other more positive influences at the orphanage that brought him a measure of comfort. The orphanage chapel, with its songs of faith, would help relieve some of Harold's fears and resentments.

HAROLD: Every Sunday we had church there. We always went. Chapel was compulsory. I called it the "church of all beliefs." It wasn't a specific denomination. It was all us kids—like a couple Chinese kids, a couple black kids, and most of us white kids and different nationalities—it was like a universe. Anyway, they had like a regular preacher who would come in there all the time and preach on Sunday. Then they had a guest preacher sometimes, and I remember hearing some sermons that were really hellfire and brimstone—nothing too heavy. But Sunday morning was a big thing. I used to like to wear clean clothes when I was a kid, and we always got nice and clean and dressed up for church.

And I loved the hymns that they sang, like "Jesus loves me, this I know, for the Bible tells me so." I loved songs like that, and I loved to sing them. But I guess nothing really stuck. You know what I mean, Dr. Sam?

Dr. Sam: In spite of this positive remembrance in Harold's reflections, the negative influences were continuously reinforced by Miss Banderhoff's terrifying punishments.

Harold: When I would misbehave or do something wrong, whatever it was, Miss Banderhoff would take me upstairs to this big attic with boxes and dolls and cans and tins—all kinds of mysterious stuff was stored up there—and she'd march me up there holding my arm, and I would plead, "Oh please, I'll be good. I'll never do it again. Oh, please, please, send me for a beating, but please, please don't lock me in the attic!" She never listened to my appeal but would take me up there, and I'd ask, "When am I going to come out?" And she'd say, "You stay on the wishing rug, and you just keep on wishing to come out." Then she would turn off the light, lock me in, and walk away!

The "wishing rug" was a rug on the floor right by the door, and I'd lie on that rug in the dark attic for what seemed like all night. I was terrified of the dark, and I thought that there was like ghosts in there. I heard little sounds of mice and I thought things were after me, and I would cry and pray and pray and say, "God, please have her come up and let me out of the attic." Then, who knows, whatever time had passed—it seemed like an eternity to me—she'd come up and let me out, give me a threat, and say, "You be good, Harold, or else!"

I was locked in that attic a lot, not just once or five times but lots of times. She was cruel, and I hated her for it. I really did. God knows I hated her for it.

Dr. Sam: Taken from his home, stripped of his identity, and punished perversely—young Harold had learned a harsh lesson: there are times when life isn't fair and people can be cruel.

Chapter 2

The Problem with Intimacy

Real intimacy touches and heals the soul.

DR. SAM: Abandonment can lead to a posttraumatic stress disorder that interferes in forming primary relationships throughout life. Such pronounced abandonment, as Harold experienced, results in anxiety; extreme sensitivity; insecurity in social life; anger with authority figures; self-defeating behaviors; and an excessive need for acceptance, approval, and control.

Harold would manifest all of the above, and though his story of abandonment and abuse is extreme, there are many elements which parallel our own lives. External circumstances and persons can force us into situations that are painful and unfair and eventually can create a platform for our own destructive behaviors. So what do we do with these experiences? And when the impact of these negative experiences is acute, as in Harold's case, is it even possible to recover?

HAROLD: My mother told me that my father was always drinking—six months drunk and six months sober. The only memory that I have of my father is that he came up and visited us one day; it was either Theodore's birthday or my birthday, I really don't remember. But he came up, and I remember that he had an old hat on, the kind of hat like one of those old hats…straw hats—flat straw hats.

He sat there with us and gave us this cake, and we were playing, and I felt so good that he was there. It is just a vague memory, but I remember throwing the hat—playing catch with the hat—I threw the hat and hit his eye and he started to cry, and I thought I'd hurt him. Then I realized that he was just crying. He was looking at us, his children who were in this orphanage, and he was crying and saying he missed us, he loved us, and he wanted us. That's the only time I ever saw him. I really don't remember how I heard when he died. I think someone came up to the home and told me my father died, but he died when I was there, and I remember them saying that it was a suicide or something like that, and that really…really made me sad.

DR. SAM: With the death of his father, Harold lost all hope that he would be able to leave the orphanage and return home. The orphanage had become a prison; he now felt completely abandoned. Sadly, Harold's experience is replicated by the millions. True, today we understand better the serious implications of separating children from their parents, and the good social worker goes to heroic efforts to maintain the family stasis. But the pandemic breakdown of the family in the United States has resulted in a stunningly high percentage of children living in single-parent families, resulting in children who are frequently unsupervised, hungry, truant, and vulnerable to sexual abuse. And so it was for Harold, in extremis.

HAROLD: There was another woman there, a matron. She was like an assistant to Miss B, as we called Miss Banderhoff. She was thin and skinny, and I liked her but I was frightened of her because there was something very strange about her. I remember some winter mornings she used to wake me up very early, and she would like pick me up out of bed. There was no one else and all the kids were in the dorm, and she would pick me up and she would say, "Okay, come on, Harold, you're going to have to go out and shovel snow." I felt like such a big guy! But then she would take me into the bathroom and fill the tub with water, and she would tell me to get in and say, "I'm going to give you a bath." I'd get in and I was naked, and she would wash me. I could have washed myself. I wasn't that small, you know, about five or six years old or so. I didn't know her and she used to play with me, and I used to get excited and I felt so exposed. I was helpless. I felt naked. I was ashamed. I was so scared. I felt powerless. I'd look at her and look at her, and she just had this funny smile on her face while she was washing me, and I felt scared.

DR. SAM: Harold was betrayed by the very person he trusted the most. A false, perverted intimacy had been substituted for a true, healthy intimacy. True intimacy is that close feeling in our personal relationships of belonging. It requires dialogue, vulnerability, and reciprocity. It results in detailed knowledge of a person's thoughts, feelings, and confidences. In healthy relationships, a deep affection or even love may result from the intimate rapport that develops. Unfortunately, Harold experienced an abusive intimacy—an intimacy twisted by his caregiver's selfish desires. Sadly, the abuse had only begun.

HAROLD: I remember one time I was downstairs in the cellar and in the storage room. There was one of the guys down there, he must have been fifteen or sixteen. I don't remember his name or even what he looked like. I just remember his fishy, scaly skin. I walked in there, or he called me in or something. I went in there and we were talking, and he started to abuse me. The next thing I knew, it was dark. I was scared, Jesus. I didn't want him to do that to me. Then what happened is, he just took me, and I was like a helpless, broken rag whimpering and suffering, and he took me and threw me in the corner and gave me a kick and said, "You tell anybody, and I'll kill you." I was terrified, and every time I saw him, I was scared that he was going to hurt me all over again.

DR. SAM: Rape is an assault on the body and psyche that is incalculable in its damage. It too is pandemic in our culture, with the Centers for Disease Control estimating nearly two million rapes per annum, mostly against women. It is little wonder that Harold developed a fear of positive intimacy later on in his life and engaged repeatedly in destructive behavior as he searched for acceptance and personal validation. This child—deprived of his home, name, and dignity—routinely experienced horrific sexual abuse, inevitably taking a tragic toll.

HAROLD: I remember one time it was a Sunday afternoon and I was at the cottage, and there was a bunch of us. We were in the dorm, and it was late Sunday afternoon, about five or six o'clock. The sun was just going down, when all of a sudden, they gathered around some of us and they started talking about sex and they wanted to do things. All of a sudden, before I knew it, I was overwhelmed. I was in the middle of a circle with all these big guys around me. They made me...they made me...

I was so ashamed, Dr. Sam, I was so ashamed. It was like the lowest spot of my life. These guys were degrading me. I was scared, and I felt humiliated. I felt I was the lowest scum in the world.

DR. SAM: What they made Harold do is unconscionable. In all of my years in private practice, I had not heard of such flagrant, coercive, sexual abuse. And yet our culture is replete with similar examples, from the cleric's anteroom to the casting director's couch, and often with irreversible consequences.

Back in California, as I transcribed the audio cassettes, I envisioned Harold sitting alone in his tiny room at the Lamb's, recalling the horrors of his abuse, and I had to question if he would ever be able to forgive himself and forgive those who had abused him so mercilessly.

HAROLD: I always had a terror and a fear that people would find out what happened—that I was raped. And I was so terrified that someone would find out that I had been forced to do these awful sexual acts, and I had this fear that if I was exposed, then I would be completely abandoned. They would send me away from the home. But where would they send me, I wondered. To another country? Or would they send me to some kind of a cruel prison, a prison for bad kids like me?

DR. SAM: For many years to come, Harold would fail to understand the linkage between his fear and shame and the subsequent violent responses he would have toward others. He's not alone. Many abused persons who engage in post-trauma destructive behavior either *don't* relate it to the trauma or justify it *because* of the trauma. It is unusual to understand thoroughly what happens in trauma—to eventually forgive the offenders and, ultimately, to forgive oneself and take responsibility for one's own unhealthy reactions.

Having been so devastatingly abused, the "fight or flight" response was already embedded in Harold's behavior, and healthy intimacy would continue to be elusive.

Chapter 3

Fighting to Survive

To live is more than to survive;
To live is to live abundantly.

DR. SAM: A natural response to abandonment and abuse can be depression and withdrawal, or it can be in doing "whatever it takes to survive." Harold chose to act out his anger with rebellion and fighting. With each passing year in the orphanage, he became more defiant and violent, achieving some measure of self-protection and self-esteem in the process. Isn't it ironic that the very tactics we use to protect and promote ourselves are the same ones that keep us from receiving the love and support necessary for our healing?

HAROLD: There was a woman there in the cottage, and her name was Miss Jones. She was the music teacher, and she loved that I sang so good and she'd give me private lessons. I had such a high voice, and she was so proud of my voice. Then I remember my friends were teasing me, "Oh, you sing like a girl," and they made fun of me! So I stopped singing high and I made my voice change on purpose, and Miss Jones knew what I was pulling.

She would say, "You sing right, Harold!" She was also teaching me how to play the piano, and I would say, "I can't." She knew I was lying, but I wanted to have the approval of my friends. I didn't want them to make fun of me and my sweet, little high voice. So after a while, she stopped giving me lessons. I really liked Miss Jones. She took an interest in me, and I liked that. But then it stopped.

DR. SAM: Here was an opportunity for Harold to have healthy intimacy and positive reinforcement from someone who accepted him as he was and wanted to help him. But his strong need for peer approval overrode that opportunity. At the same time, his anger toward those who had abused him was festering.

HAROLD: When I was being abused, I felt this tremendous shame, deep down inside my heart. There was an anger, a revenge, and a tenacity that said, "You dirty ————. Someday I'm going to get revenge on you. You're tough now. You're stronger than me. You abuse me. You hurt me. You humiliate me. You shame me. But someday, I'm going to grow up. Someday I'm going to be tougher than you. Someday I'll do and hurt you the way you did to me, you dirty ————." I didn't say it out loud, but it was in my heart. As I was being humiliated, I made a vow. I was determined that someday I would be tougher and I would do to them what they did to me.

There was this guy, Ernie, there at the home, and he was one of the most respected guys there. He came from Brooklyn. He was talking about how you got to be tough, you've got to be hard. He punched somebody out in the dorm, and everybody feared him. Everybody respected him. I wanted to be this guy's friend. I wanted to be the tough guy's friend. I was so scared. I was like the smallest kid there, and I wanted to be like these guys that were so strong and tough. I used to say, someday, I'll be strong and tough like them, but I knew I wasn't a strong or tough guy. I was a scared, timid guy. But deep down, I wanted to be tough because I wanted the respect that they had.

DR. SAM: Harold's true nature and personality—a sensitive, shy boy with a soprano voice—were being manipulated and morphed into a "tough guy," the only role he could play that provided him some esteem and accolades from his tough-guy role models. Harold was now ready to enter the ring, surrounded by the cheering admiration of his peers.

HAROLD: I don't know who it was. It was Richard Banning, I think. Yeah, it was Richard. I had a fight with Richard in this big bathroom. I was so scared, but we started fighting, and they made a big circle around us, and Richard was beating me up. Boy, he was beating me. I was trying to box and jab, but he was the one hitting me, and I was scared and shaking inside. I was losing, when all of a sudden this one guy walked into the room as we were fighting, and he was standing on the side, and he said, "Come on, Harold, beat him up. Get that Greek temper up and beat him up." For him, I wanted to have courage for his approval. Boy, I was so proud that this guy looked at me and said, "Come on, kid, you can beat him up." I tore into Banning, and I beat him, I beat him bad. It wasn't my strength. I needed the encouragement. I appreciated that. Someone finally gave a damn about me and believed in me. I always wanted that.

DR. SAM: Harold finally felt like he belonged. He had fought back. He had gotten even. He had proved himself a man and earned the respect and approval of his peers and role models. But the deeper, underlying issues remained untouched. Because of the ongoing abuse he was experiencing at the orphanage, Harold was like the proverbial cat cornered by the big bad dog—tired of hissing and pawing, the combative cat jumps over the dog and takes flight. Harold had chosen to fight repeatedly, but the impulse to run was also present and he would act on it.

HAROLD: I ran away from the home, and I was really, really proud because my brother Theodore was older and tougher than me, he was a natural fighter, and he never ran away, though my other older brother, Basil, did run away. He was at the orphanage before I got there, in another cottage, and he'd run away and never did come back. He died later. He got killed. I don't know how. But me, I always wanted to go home. I always wanted to go to my mother and my father and my sisters. I wanted to get out of there, but no one ever got out of there, except my brother. I never heard of anyone else escaping and making it out. People were discharged, and they went home to their families legally.

So what happened is, I ran away and I got caught the same night. I don't remember how far I got, but I remember I got caught the same night. The punishment that I got when I got caught was, they shaved all my hair and gave me "a baldy," and they didn't give me no dessert for a week and no movies for a month. Of course, they sent me to Dr. M. (the Headmaster), and he gave me a beating. He would hit us with a big paddling board with holes in it. Sometimes he would miss your fanny and smack you on the back of the thighs, and it would hurt. But I was proud—proud that I was the most incorrigible boy of the year and that I got the record for the most beatings in a year; proud that I took the chance, a chance on the great adventure to try and get home to my mother and my family. And all the kids, my friends there at the orphanage, they really loved me for trying and they understood. They were proud that I ran away. Three times I tried to run away, and the staff would shave my head each time. That bald head became a badge of honor, a badge of honor because I had become tough and had defied authority.

DR. SAM: Harold had taken on a new identity, assuming the persona of a rebellious tough guy. He had transitioned from fear of peer reprisals to confidence in his strength to fight and inflict pain on others. And by defying authority, he had won approval. This new persona would prove to be Harold's modus operandi for years to come, and it would be the driving force after his transition back into the larger community. It would eventually prove a dangerous persona to play.

Chapter 4

Going Home

Life's journey is about finding your way home.

DR. SAM: Harold wanted nothing more than to leave the orphanage and "get home to mama." And even though his peers respected him for beating up Richard and attempting to run away, they continued to taunt him.

HAROLD: You know, kids are cruel. They made up jingles and sang, "When the moon shines green on Harold's baldy bean, that's where the cooties love to play. La, la, la." They made fun of me, but in a way, they really liked me. They danced around and sang, making fun of my bald head.

DR. SAM: Nor did Harold ever make peace with his nemesis, Miss Banderhoff. She had taken away his name, imposed punitive measures for the least offense, and had repeatedly thrown him into the attic. More than anything, though, he resented "Miss B" for pretending to be his surrogate mother. That resentment sought retribution, and Harold would wait patiently for years until that long-anticipated moment came.

HAROLD: I was twelve, and finally, one day they just told me. They said, "Harold, you and your brother, Theodore, are going home in a week." It was very short notice. They said it was a week or a couple of days that we were going to go. This was my lifelong dream, and I was, like, thrilled. I remember running to see Theodore—"We're going home! We're going home!" We danced, and I said, "Gee, I'll see you tomorrow!" We were so excited!

All my friends were coming over to me now. I was there at the home almost eight years, and all my friends were so excited. "Harold, you're going home, you're going home!" They wanted to go home too, you know. I'm sure that in their eyes they saw in me what they always wanted—to go home! Of course, I was going to miss them. These were my friends. These were the only people I knew, yet I wanted to go. I wanted to leave them all. I wanted to go home. There was no question about that. It was my dream finally come true. I was going home with my brother! I think that it was in a couple days the notice came that we were going to go, and I was so excited and so happy!

DR. SAM: Harold's greatest wish had come true. Unfortunately, on what should have been an exclusively joyous occasion, Harold's resentments came to the surface, and he was incapable of not acting on them.

HAROLD: I didn't want to look at Miss Banderhoff. I didn't want to talk to her. I didn't want to see her. I was finally going to leave her grasp, her power, her control. She had no more power over me. It was official. I was going, and it was my turn. In my way, it was my turn to hit back at her. I never could ever hit back or say anything back, talk back. I had no power, and now I was going. Now I finally had some power. My power was not to say a word to her. It was my way of getting back. Now I'm going to get you back. I didn't even want to acknowledge her, look at her. She was nothing to me. I just ignored her completely. That was my way of hitting back at her. I enjoyed doing it. I wanted to do it, and I did it.

DR. SAM: Powerless for so many years, here was Harold's opportunity to assert power and gain control. In different ways, we all can identify. Many of us have experienced issues of abandonment and abuse: An alcoholic father who has been emotionally absent from our life. A domineering mother who prefers physical punishment to care and reason. A child who has left home, never to return or communicate again. A spouse of many years who vanishes from our life. A lover who leaves us for another. A relative's sexual abuse. A coworker's predatory behavior. The list goes on and on of the many ways in which we have all felt powerless. Few of us, though, act out as Harold did in his passive-aggressive response to Miss B.

HAROLD: It was a Saturday, or was it Sunday? We were getting ready to leave, and my brother came to the cottage to pick me up, and Miss Banderhoff laid out the clothes and stuff. But I just didn't pay attention to her. I just washed and got dressed. I never even acknowledged her. I never looked at her. I avoided her completely. She'd talk, and I'd just look. I didn't even respond.

All my friends were there, and they were hugging and kissing me. It was like a big occasion when someone left, you know. It was like the biggest occasion in my life. I was saying, "Goodbye, goodbye," and everyone was saying, "Come on, you've got to hurry, hurry, and get to the bus out in front."

I started to walk away, all of a sudden, I heard, "Harold!" It was Miss B. It was her voice, and she was at the top of the stairs. She looked at me, and she opened her eyes wide and said, "Aren't you going to say good-bye to me?" Like, you know, come run into my arms, little darling, and give me a kiss. It was my chance, and I looked at her and I spit on the floor. I just spit, and I turned my back on her and walked out, and I left and I didn't turn back. It was my way of saying, "You dirty ————! You ————! I'm glad I'm away from you and I won't be around you anymore. All the years you hurt me. *You* were *cruel* to me, and now you want me to kiss you goodbye?" I didn't plan it, but it was in my heart. That's what I did. I just spit and turned around.

Now, I had the power. It was the first time I could defy her, and I stood up to her and I knew there was going to be no retaliation. I was going home to my family and my mother, and me and Theodore walked down that road, and I was proud and happy. All my friends were yelling, "Harold! Harold! Harold!" I got my revenge with all the surliness that was within me.

As soon as we got on the bus, we took out our hankies, and—I'll never forget this—we wiped the dust off our shoes. We wiped the home off us. We wiped the dust off our shoes, and we looked at each other, and we smiled and laughed, "Ha-ha!" We were away after all those years, and we were going home!

DR. SAM: Who can blame Harold for his animus toward Miss B and his "surly," dramatic exit from the orphanage? He certainly felt justified, with a tone of self-righteous indignation in his voice: "We wiped the dust off our shoes! We wiped the home off us!" Unconsciously, Harold was imitating Christ's disciples as they shook the dust from their sandals when leaving a town that had not welcomed them.

But as I listen again to Harold's words from nearly fifty years ago, might it be that the "seeds of forgiveness" had been planted by the very person whom he perceived as his nemesis?

HAROLD: I remember at Christmastime, we would all gather around, and Miss B would make hot chocolate and she'd play the piano and we'd sing Christmas carols. Boy, it was really good, and I loved those carols! And every Christmas Eve, we had this ritual. Miss B would make this big Christmas cake 'cause it was Jesus's birthday. And what we did was, we carried the cake in a procession. She would lead the way, and then the one that had been in the home the longest would carry the cake with two hands, and all the kids would line up behind him. Each kid had a candle, and the cake was lit, and we walked in procession, and it was like we were saying, "Glory to God, Happy Birthday, Jesus!" We walked all through the house, even up to the attic, and then came down and all had a piece of cake and sang carols to Jesus. I remember it was always my dream that someday my turn would come to carry the cake.

But then, after being there at Russell Cottage for five years, I was sent to Perkins Cottage for a year, so now I came back right before Christmas, and it was time for whoever was in the home the longest to carry the cake. Now I had really been there the longest; but because I left for a year, when we all lined up for the Christmas cake procession, I got in the line last because I was like the fresh guy in the cottage. I was there for so long but had just come back.

So I got way on the end of the line, and they got the cake and they lit it up with the candles. All of a sudden, Miss B said, "Where's Harold?" Someone says, "He's at the end of the line." And she said, "Get up here and carry the cake, Harold!" I almost dropped dead. I didn't expect it. I couldn't believe that I was going to carry the cake! I was so proud to be carrying Jesus's birthday cake!

DR. SAM: In spite of this fond memory, Harold had no illusions about Miss Banderhoff, recording at one point, "She was really nice at Christmas time. She was not herself. I mean, she showed affection at times, and I'm sure she loved us in her own sick, sick way." But it was this positive remembrance of her calling on him to carry the Christmas cake that empowered Harold to embrace a more fully human portrait of Miss B. And perhaps, even among Harold's painful memories of abuse, it is out of this warm recollection that those seeds of forgiveness began to flourish.

HAROLD: Whoever is listening to this tape or reading these words may think I'm a kid, but that's okay. I just was so proud to be picked to carry the cake for Christ's birthday. It was a special blessing to me, and even right now, it's a blessing to these painful memories, Dr. Sam. I have to thank Miss B for letting me carry the cake. And I have to thank you for that, dear God, for using her as a-an instrument in my life. Bless, Miss Banderhoff, dear God, bless her.

DR. SAM: As our story unfolds, we will better understand the aspiration inherent in Harold's simple prayer versus the virtual hell on earth he had yet to travel. But for now, all was well. Harold was going home.

Anxiously, as he travels on the bus with his brother Theodore, from Spring Valley to New York City, Harold can't help but wonder, *Will anyone be there to meet me? Is mama going to be there?* His question is in some way our question: *Will there be anyone to welcome us home?*

Chapter 5

Family and Friends

With friends like these, who needs enemies.
—Anonymous

DR. SAM: Harold's dream was about to come true. What he had hoped for, prayed for, ran away for, and fought for would soon be a reality. He was going home. But his concern about anyone being there to meet him at the bus station was a valid one. In Harold's eight years at the orphanage, his mother, brothers, and sisters would visit him a total of six times.

HAROLD: Every Sunday morning was visiting day, and I used to look out the window and just wait because there was never any communication from home. There was never a letter. I don't even think I ever got a phone call or nothing. I never knew when they were going to come, so I'd always wait and think maybe mother would come. Every once in a while, someone would say, "Maybe this is the Sunday your mom will come." They never told me when they were going to come. You just got a call when they were there, and the staff would say, "Hey, your mother's here." You know it was like a big shock. I mean, I got less than one visit a year. After a while, you got so that you didn't look anymore.

DR. SAM: This protracted emotional estrangement from his family exacerbated the initial sense of abandonment Harold felt when he was abruptly sent to the orphanage. On an elementary level, he understood the reason he had been sent to the home but inevitably questioned his mother's love for him.

HAROLD: She was powerless to take us home. She really had no choice, no money. This was in the 1930s, Dr. Sam, the depression was still going on, and she couldn't feed her kids. She had no husband. The welfare people had control of her situation. The court insisted some of us go to the children's home. They would withhold her money if we didn't. It hurt her, of course, but I didn't understand that, and I deep down felt that maybe she didn't care. It hurt me, and I felt unlovable. If my mother didn't want me and my father, then I was unlovable, or "unwantable." That's what I felt. I felt unwantable. No one loved me, and I couldn't love myself.

Yet I loved her, and all I wanted was to be home again. We would all be together again. It would be so nice.

DR. SAM: Even now, on the biggest day of his life, full of the excitement and anticipation of being reunited with his family, Harold couldn't help but be fearful, full of self-doubt, and mistrust. Would he be accepted by his family, meet with their approvable? Would he be "wantable" enough, lovable enough? And, yes, that gnawing question he'd ask himself over and over on that anxious bus ride into the city, Would there be anyone there to welcome him home?

HAROLD: We got off the bus at Penn Station with two little suitcases. We were like lost kids. And then, who was there to welcome us home but Steven, my oldest brother! It was Steven standing right there! He said, "Come on!" and we hopped a cab or whatever. It was the biggest day of our lives! Here I was in the big city, and the cars, and the honking, and the noise, and the people. And it was, like, overwhelming. And we're looking around the city when we come up to Tenth Street where my mother lived all these years, and there was, like, people from the block there. They must have known. It was like a big event. And then we went upstairs, and I got in the house, and then…then I hugged my mother. I hugged my mother, and she hugged me! And, boy, I remember she made spaghetti. We had a big spaghetti dinner! And my sister Jena was there, and my older sister Elena and Steven was so proud to have us home. And Momma was so proud, and I was looking at them, and they were looking at me and Theodore. And I knew they loved me and that I loved them, and I knew that I was home!

DR. SAM: One could only hope that the support of his family might give Harold the affirmation and security he needed. And if "home *is* where the heart is," Harold unreservedly brought his heart from the orphanage to his family home. Yet not unlike the fear he faced when entering the orphanage, Harold would soon realize that his real family were like strangers to him. Even so, his deep need for their acceptance and love fueled his belief that they loved one another unconditionally and that he was safely "home" at last.

Regrettably, Harold didn't realize that the imprinted behavioral patterns from the orphanage would contaminate his relationships with family and friends for years to come. Harold had survived eight years in a dysfunctional orphanage family, only now to be faced with a dysfunctional family at home.

HAROLD: I came home to like...strangers. I mean, they were my brothers and sisters, but I didn't know anything about them. I didn't know any of them, really, including my mother! I loved her, and yet, you know, I was always wondering if she loved me, if she'd changed. I mean, I knew she loved me—you know when someone loves you—but I always had that mistrust. Does she really care? It was ingrained in me.

Some days I'd act sick and say, "I can't go to school. I'm sick, Mother," and she'd be nice and give me special attention. I wanted a mother all over again, a real relationship. When she'd go to the store, I'd say, "Mom, I'll go with you." The city was so scary to me, but I'd go down with her and, at twelve years old, I'd hold her hand. I remember a couple of kids on the block who said, "What are you holding your mother's hand for?" But to me, she was like a brand-new mother, and this was the first time I could walk with her and hold her hand, and I was so happy to be with her!

Theodore was older and rougher and after the first week home was already hanging out and running around the streets with Steven. Unless I was with Mama, I would just sit home and be scared—scared of the city, the neighborhood, the bigger kids. I was like in a brand-new, big world and I was terrified inside.

DR. SAM: Harold is not the first one to cower behind closed doors after being released from the restraints of a confining institution. The unfettered possibilities of freedom can create acute anxiety, causing in many a prison of fear. Thousands of men, women, and children released from homeless shelters, orphanages, refugee camps, prisons, and mental institutions struggle with the challenges of re-assimilating back into the broader culture. Had eight years of psychological and physical abuse left Harold irreparably damaged? Would the semblance of a normal home be sufficient to give him a positive sense of who he was and what he could achieve? Or would fear paralyze Harold from getting out of the apartment into this scary brand-new, big world?

HAROLD: Slowly, I started playing with the kids on the block and getting to know them a little bit. They all knew my brother Steven and the family. They said, "Hey, you're Harold, you're the country hick." They called me hick, and then because I was like a little chubby, they started calling me Butterball. They'd say, "Hey, he's like a little butterball," and it started bothering me. They didn't call me by my name, Harold—they called me Butterball. I wanted to be friends with them, you know, but I was scared in the beginning. It took a real long time 'cause they were all rough kids, street kids. Man, they'd talk nasty and loud, and they'd run around and yell at people. They'd defy people. It wasn't like in the home, you know. If you ever did things like that, you'd get killed, thrown in the attic! But they'd scream at cars and yell like little street urchins. I'd look at them in amazement. They were rough. They frightened me, and yet I liked them. But they always teased me, calling me hick and Butterball, and I'd get angry that they made fun of me because I was chubby.

DR. SAM: Once again, Harold felt the insult, pain, and resultant anger of being called a name other than his own. "Riley," "Hick," and "Butterball" didn't represent his core identity. But Harold's deep need for acceptance produced a near insatiable desire for friendship.

HAROLD: My main interest in life was my friends. They were more important than my family. They were more important than anybody. I made friends with Elliot and Luke, and Andre the Bog and Damion B, and Freddie B and Xander, and the other kids on the block. We all went to PS 122. They were tough kids and I was scared, but we just hung out, the Tenth Street kids and me. We'd play stickball and stuff, and we used to sneak into the movies and we would rob hot bread from the bakery, and a couple of times we hitched a ride on the trolley. My attitude was mostly to be accepted and to get along and to impress.

DR. SAM: A fearful twelve-year-old Harold would *do* anything, *become* anything to be accepted. This compulsion to "go along with the crowd"—how frequently we see it acted out today by young people from all different social strata (the rampant bullying in our schools; the hazing, even to the point of death, in our college fraternities). Not unlike the pressure Harold felt to impress the Tenth Street kids, adolescents today experience inordinate pressure to excel—to be the top student, the best athlete—resulting in a teen suicide rate that is at record high. In fact, a 2017 study reports that suicide is the second leading cause of death among teenagers.

What is the inordinate peer pressure in our lives that drives so many of us into destructive behavioral patterns? In Harold's case, he would soon resort to those old patterns encouraged by a member of his own family!

HAROLD: I didn't realize it then, but I hero-worshiped my brother Steven. When I went to PS 64 at around fourteen, the attitude was, you got to be a tough guy. Steven kept telling me, "You gotta be tough, Harold. You gotta be a fighter." That's all I heard, "You've got to be tough to be accepted." And I was scared because I knew I wasn't tough. My biggest fear was that I'd show somebody that I was scared, that I wasn't tough. That was my biggest fear. So I kept trying to be tough. I had to be strong.

DR. SAM: Harold would go to considerable efforts to project that tough-guy image: He began subscribing to muscle magazines. He'd go to the park and do laps in the pool. He'd lift weights with his buddies Elliot and Luke, work out in the gym daily, even become a fighter like his brother Theodore, only to be knocked out in the third round of his boxing debut. But Harold wouldn't stay down for long. He was always getting up, punching back, striving, his objective clear.

HAROLD: I wanted to stand out. That's what I really wanted. I wanted to be above the crowd and be different. The people who were talked about the most in the school— the tough guys.

DR. SAM: The tough-guy persona that was planted in the orphanage was now being perfected. But it was never enough. It never is. Harold would have to prove himself time and again.

HAROLD: I started to rob kids of their lunch money. I would shake them down. I would smack them around. I had some kids I used to bulldog, and I'd say, "If you don't give me a nickel a day, I'll give you a beating."

DR. SAM: As time went on, Harold began hanging out at the pool hall with a group of kids known as the Sixth Street Boys, a.k.a., "Satan's Boys." Alex was their leader. He was a big, strong young man who liked to fight. Naturally, he and Harold became good friends, and they began doing crazy things together.

HAROLD: One night we went down to the local park (my voice drops, Dr. Sam, because I'm ashamed), me, Alex, and another guy, Jason F, and any guy we saw we hit. We had a contest to see between the three of us who could punch the hardest. So every guy we came across, we punched. So, we'd say, "Alex, see if you can knock this guy out that's coming." They'd just be walking through the park, and Alex would walk over, and *boom*, the guy would go down. If he wasn't knocked out, they'd say, "Hey, Harold," and I'd hit the next guy. That night alone we dropped thirteen guys.

Dr. Sam: Within a couple of years, Harold had gone from a petty shakedown artist to a dangerous stalker of the vulnerable.

Harold: We hit bums. We hit regular men, older men, young men. We just were crazy, and we were asserting our power. I always felt, you know, that I was powerless, and now I could punch someone and knock them down. They used to call me crazy, and I loved the reputation. If I didn't knock someone out, I felt unsure, unsteady. Then I would knock somebody down, and I would feel like I was, "Okay. I've still got some power. I'm all right." I'm not scared anymore.

Dr. Sam: Once let loose, violence has a voracious appetite; and with every punch thrown, Harold was delivering "payback" for all the pain he had received as a child. When he was nearly sixteen, his mother remarried and moved out of the apartment, leaving Harold alone once more—this time, with his older brothers, Theodore and Steven. Theodore soon joined the army where he honed his boxing skills, and Steven was absent most of the time with a very busy nightlife. Harold, left to his own devices, took up mugging to make a living; then, over time, he would graduate to more sophisticated, well-planned stickups.

Harold: At night I looked to rob somebody. I beat people up and hurt them unmercifully, and then took their wallets and ran. Soon, though, as I got older, I was planning stickups. And that became my whole life. Me, Christopher, and Sebastian, and this guy, Tim Damario—we were like the first guys in my crowd that started going on stickups. I remember I just loved following guys, like someone on a payroll run, and watching them go to the bank and going back to the place. Them not knowing that I was following them, and me knowing gave me a sense of power and mystery and intrigue. It was like a great adventure, it was like I was a spy. The adrenaline…it thrilled me, not like sexual but it was like a very emotionally fulfilling and exciting adventure like you were going on a combat mission. I really loved it, carrying a pistol and the risk of doing something illegal and maybe getting caught. The closer the time came to the stickup, I would get tremendously apprehensive and nervous.

DR. SAM: Rather than have a drink to steel himself before a stickup, Harold found an unusual way to calm his nerves. It would be a portent of things to come.

HAROLD: I'd have to have a pint of ice cream before we'd go on a stickup. It just would make me feel calm and settle me. I had to have it. It meant love to me or some kind of security blanket. It calmed the anxiety. Before the stickup, I used to lick my double-scoop ice cream in the back of the car and sing that song, "I'll go from rags to riches. I'll be a king."

DR. SAM: With ice cream as his antidote for anxiety, the violent stickups would accelerate. Harold, always looking for newer "role models," would begin to admire some new tough guys in the neighborhood, the "wise guys" whom he didn't want to mess with yet still wanted to emulate.

HAROLD: I'd heard about them. I didn't know them personally, but I saw them around the neighborhood, and they
hung out at Fox's Corner, and everybody said these
were the guys in the Mafia. They walked around with
brand-new suits, and everybody talked about them with
tremendous respect and fear. It was brought up that if
you ever messed with them, they'd kill you. The greatest
thing that could ever come to you was to be in their
favor. I didn't trust them, but I wanted their approval or
at least a pat on the back.

DR. SAM: Emboldened by his previous success and wanting
the respect of the Mafia, Harold was on the lookout for
his next impressive heist.

HAROLD: I was so sure of this one. A guy who worked for
the Howard Clothing Factory in Brooklyn gave us a
payroll tip. So me, Christopher, Sebastian, and this guy
Damion (our getaway driver), we go to Brooklyn to
case it: Every morning this employee drives to the bank,
picks up the payroll in a briefcase, and comes out of the
bank with a guard dressed in regular civilian clothes.
(We'd been tipped off that he carries a pistol.) Then
they get into their car and drive to a parking lot, then
cross the street, and then walk on over to the factory.
Now that we knew their routine, we made a plan and
went back to Brooklyn for the actual stickup.

Sebastian and Christopher walked behind the
two guys 'til they got to the corner where Damion had
parked the car. I'm coming in from the front, walking
toward the guys to meet them in front of the car, and,
with Sebastian and Christopher's help, will push them
into the car. I had it all timed out, and as I'm walking
toward them with my hand on the pistol, Sebastian and
Christopher start waving their arms like, "It's all off! It's

all off!" I'm saying to myself, "It's too late. I can't stop," and so I take the pistol out of my pocket and strike the armed guard in the head and he goes right down. Then I hit the other guy as Sebastian and Christopher come running over, and we start punching and pistol—whipping these two guys, and I just keep slapping the guard's face with the pistol—crack, crack, crack.

We picked up the briefcase, got in the car, and took off screaming, leaving them bleeding. We went only a few blocks and spotted this cab following us and jumped out of the car, and we're in Brooklyn on this avenue and there's no way out. There's only a fence and water down where the docks are, but somehow Damion gets away. Sebastian, me, and Christopher are roaming the streets when the cops arrive, circle us, move in, and arrest us. Of course, they questioned us right away. Me, wanting to be a hero, tried to take the rap, saying, "It was all my idea."

DR. SAM: The police weren't buying Harold's last-minute heroics. Eventually, all three were convicted. Damion was never caught or "ratted on" by the others. At the trial, Harold was sentenced to ten years.

From the sixth floor of the Lamb's, in a high-pitched, muffled voice, Harold speaks softly into the tape recorder as he reflects on his life of crime: "I hated myself for doing those things. What I really felt was that I hated what was in me, what was compelling me to do them."

The tragic through line of Harold's life may seem inexorable. One could persuasively argue that he was destined for a life of criminal depravity. But that leads us to ask, Where were the mentors when he needed them the most? Where were the *positive* role models? Where was a loving, supportive father? Where was the much-needed intervention from a caring family member or a concerned pastor? And finally, after years of poisonous abuse in the orphanage, could the prison system restore Harold to health, or would this be the incarceration that would destroy him?

Street where Harold lived.

Local park where Harold did his mugging?

Chapter 6

Imprisoned Again

In solitary confinement, nothing is unimaginable.

DR. SAM: Harold's journey from petty criminal to major felon is not atypical. Of the nearly 2.3 million men incarcerated in America's prisons, many of them have travelled a similar path. What is atypical is the level of *wanton* violence that Harold's criminal behavior reached. At one point, Harold and his friend Jordi pummeled a harmless man on a Brooklyn subway and gave him a send-off.

HAROLD: Boom, boom, boom, boom, and the guy falls right by the door. And as soon as the train pulls into the station, as the door opens, we roll him out and gave him a send-off. We rolled him right out of the car and left him on the platform, and the doors closed and everybody in the car was looking at us shocked. They didn't say a word—it was so violent. We looked around. My adrenaline was pumping. I was excited, I was nervous, I was scared, and I was all hopped up, and Jordi looked at me and says, "You want to give these other guys a send-off too?" He looked at the whole car. I said, "Sure, let's go."

DR. SAM: And they did, randomly punching out as many people in the car as they could before it pulled into to the next station where those passengers still standing fled in terror.

In spite of this sociopathic behavior, Harold was not a remorseless monster. He was aware of his condition. He often described himself as "cruel and sick." He had a functioning conscience, and shortly before that final stickup, he took a positive step and sought help.

HAROLD: I admit I was sick. I was very sick, and one night I was lying in bed, and I started feeling strange and guilty about all the robbing and the mugging, and I don't know what I was going through. I felt my body was raising up out of me, and I ended up going to the hospital. I just went down there, met a psychiatrist, and admitted myself. I stayed there at Bellevue around three months—October, November, and part of December. It was 1952.

DR. SAM: Once again, at Bellevue, Harold found himself in a structured environment, which paradoxically gave him a sense of disquieting comfort.

HAROLD: It's a funny thing about community. When I was in the home, I was in community. In some ways, Bellevue was like that—the wards, the beds. There was guys, and we talked. It was secure, and I was fed. But I was disturbed, upset, and I ran away—escaped—and came home to the old neighborhood on Tenth Street.

DR. SAM: Harold's cry for help would continue. He would be a patient at Bellevue and Rockland State Hospital on three separate occasions in his late teens and early twenties, eventually giving them permission to use electroconvulsive treatments. In the 1950s, this was not an uncommon practice on those who were considered criminally incorrigible. Within weeks after those treatments, Harold was released and went right back to doing stickups, culminating in the failed Brooklyn heist that would land him in Sing Sing.

HAROLD: We called it the "big house" and the "country club on the Hudson," but it sure wasn't that. I didn't want to be there and went into a deep sulk and just kept thinking about escaping and getting out. I didn't want to adjust to this life. I was scared, nervous, depressed, and yet I was excited. I was put in with all these prisoners, and like everybody's talking about cases and robbery, and I felt like I had made it. Like I was somebody. I had gotten arrested, and getting arrested in my neighborhood and doing time was like you had arrived, you had made it—you were finally a tough guy. It was like I was a success at the criminal life. I was a con now, a big con, like in the movies, like James Cagney and Humphrey Bogart and those guys.

DR. SAM: This romanticized, self-congratulatory interlude was short-lived. At Sing Sing, there would be no pints of ice cream, no stickups with dreams of going from rags to riches overnight. The stark reality of prison soon settled in.

HAROLD: I hated the way the hacks [guards] treated me. Like dirt. You never had no freedom. You couldn't make a decision on your own. They told you to get here and there, and they talked to you like you were scum. Most of the time you was in your cell, and then it was line up here, line up there. Everything was a lineup. A typical day was like I'd get up in the morning, and I felt despair—another damned day—line up and go to the mess hall and come out and line up again and just shoot the crap with the guys. Everybody was lying to each other, looking to impress each other, most of the time talking about crime, like, continuously, all day long. Crime, crime, crime. I got so sick of crime. It got so that's all we knew. That's all they were interested in, and that's all we did. We talked about crime, crime, crime. The stickup you did. The stickup I did. The things we were going to do when we got out. Our plans to get together, and this and that. How to scheme for leaving the prison. How to break the system. How to get extra food without getting caught. How to get away with this. How to get away with that.

DR. SAM: It's little wonder that the recidivism rate of our prisons is so high. In many ways, our correctional facilities are breeding grounds for further criminality. We do a decent job at incarceration, but the challenges of effective and permanent rehabilitation are daunting. Harold and most of his fellow inmates have a distorted worldview that feeds into a delusional perception of reality. It's a twisted reality, and one that is difficult to penetrate and untangle.

HAROLD: The code I was brought up with was that if you worked, you were square. You were a John. You were the biggest creep. Only creeps went to work. The smart guys robbed. They stole, and they took from legitimate people that they considered schmucks and squares. People told me to get an education, but I was looking for a quick buck that I could spend on fancy clothes and good shiny shoes and fancy cars and, of course, women. It was, like, exciting and challenging, and this was the way it was supposed to be.

DR. SAM: With the mounting tensions of prison life, Harold's delusional view of reality would only increase. I can still hear the anxiety in his voice, as years later, Harold recalls his funny feelings about the Mafia.

HAROLD: I was in the mess hall reading the paper about this guy getting pinched, who just happened to be messed up with the Mafia, and it turns out, Dr. Sam, this guy was the same old, retired bookmaker that Jordi and me tried to rob one night! Now, I've always heard that if you fool around with the Mafia, you get killed or something. And right after reading this, I got these guilty, funny kind of thoughts that maybe I'm going to get killed by one of them. They were just very vague thoughts at the time—a nebulous, funny kind of feeling that disturbed and upset me. But this fear of getting killed sometime by the Mafia, it was like this forlorn feeling that would just sweep over me.

DR. SAM: Harold's fear of imagined threats and conspiracies were all a part of his paranoia. Occasionally, those fears would reach such intense levels that he would have psychotic reactions, manifested by hearing or seeing things that were not real. But generally, Harold was able to maintain his ability to reason and *not* become fixed in a delusional reality. His observations of the dangers of prison life were accurate. He understood that the social strata in prison is based on power, and there was no doubt in Harold's mind who occupied the top stratum, with its power to intimidate and control others.

HAROLD: The highest status in the prison was the Mafia. If a guy was a Mafia man, if he was a member of organized crime, nobody bothered him. Everybody respected them, and they stood off by themselves. They didn't hang out with anybody but themselves. They knew everybody and they were friendly with everybody, but they were approached from a distance with courtly respect. No one messed with them. No one.

Then the status in the prison went down. Next was us stickup guys, the robbers, and then the next lowest was the rats—the stool pigeon who ratted on someone. The lowest of all in the social status in prison was what we called "short heisters." These were guys that were in there for raping kids, girls or boys, and even some for animals. No one bothered with them. They were completely ostracized. They walked in the yard completely alone, except with another of their kind.

DR. SAM: As a safeguard against his fears, both phantom and real, Harold kept to himself as much as possible. In his cell, he read poetry, a little philosophy, and some Westerns and mysteries as well. He kept himself in tip-top shape lifting weights, and after being transferred to Auburn Prison for an altercation at Sing Sing, Harold won the annual arm wrestling competition against some very stiff competition. And he did make a few friends along the way.

HAROLD: Yeah, there was Lewis M, an Albanian from my neighborhood. He was an illiterate lifer for murder who had learned to read while at Auburn and then became proficient in quantum mechanics. I really loved Lou. He was brilliant. Then there was Julius, a real tough and respected guy from Brooklyn. Nobody messed with him. He had the reputation as a wild man. We gravitated toward each other. I guess it was the same thing as me and Jordi. Then I started to work out on the ditch gang, and there was a bunch of guys—Damon, Luke, Sammy—we all got along pretty good. And I believe the Lord was with me even then because He knew I really liked the outdoors, and doing hard work was a way to get the anger out. But I guess my attitude while in prison was you never could show softness. I always had to show that I was a tough guy. You could never cry—I was taught that—no softness or closeness or affection for each other. It was always like…keep your distance.

DR. SAM: Even though Harold was able to channel his anger and took pride in having had only two altercations while at Auburn Prison, he was put into solitary confinement after slugging an inmate unconscious who was gossiping about him, accusing Harold of having slept with a Mafioso's girlfriend (which he had, unknowingly!). Being thrown into "the box," as it is called, took Harold full circle emotionally, back to the terror he experienced when confined to the attic while at the orphanage, amplifying all his anxieties and fears.

HAROLD: Being in the box was not a pleasant experience. I was apprehensive, scared, and depressed, always tense. My biggest fear was that I might crack up or go crazy. I had these thoughts that someone was looking to stab me—these fearful, hallucinatory thoughts—and they scared me. Every once in a while, a guy would crack up in Auburn, and they would ship him out. And if you cracked up, you know, even if you did, like, almost your ten years but you cracked up, they would put you in a mental institution and you could never get out and that frightened me. Would I be the next one to have a crack-up?

DR. SAM: As if on cue, Harold would witness the crack-up of a fellow inmate, followed by an act of courageous concern that may have saved that inmate's life and, ultimately, Harold's.

HAROLD: He was in there for a short heist, that's what the rumor was, but Damon was liked because he was a simple, childlike guy, and was tremendously strong—the strongest guy in the prison. He could lift more weights than anybody, and he weighed like 320 lbs. He worked in the mess hall and never bothered anybody. No one messed with him or bothered to put him down because all he had to do was hit you once or squeeze you and he could crush you.

Anyway, Damon had a crack-up, and they put him in the box. The story went around that the prison doctor went into the box and talked to him and ordered some kind of sodium pentothal, something like that, and he wanted to use it on Damon to get to the subconscious—to see what was bothering him—and the prison officials said, "No, you can't." The doc said he would and threatened to take them to court and charge them with criminal negligence, saying that they were thwarting the help of an inmate and his work, and he was, like, the first guy—this young little guy from Brooklyn, this little psychologist—to stand up against the administration. At that time, I never heard of anybody, staff or administration, standing up to them. But this kind doctor; he stood up to them.

What happened is, they buckled under, and he worked with Damon and he got fine. In a few weeks' time, maybe a month or more, he got him out of the box and back into the yard. Damon came together just as good as before, and he was like a hero in the joint, and he was a hero in my eyes. And I really liked this doc. He was very calm, quiet, and kind. When he asked me if I might want some therapy, I said yeah, and I really opened up to him, and we became good friends. I think that was the first time in my life that I had a real interest in growth. Here was a man who took an interest in me, and he helped me take a...a positive interest in myself. It was just a little seed...but like a good seed.

DR. SAM: The road to health begins with one's recognition that he or she is in need of help. And like many who have profound psychological challenges, Harold had developed a well-supplied toolkit of defense mechanisms: denial, regression, acting out, dissociation, projection, repression, and rationalization were all frequently employed. Now, thanks to the concern and skillful help of a young prison psychologist, Harold was beginning to look inward, not only to understand the *why* of his behavior but to consciously alter his destructive behavioral impulses, preparing him to reenter society with a measure of health and confidence. The possibility of that reentry would come sooner than Harold anticipated.

HAROLD: So, after two years, I went to see the parole board. And shortly before I was to see them, I got into this little fight with a guy. I don't even remember what it was about. The doc said to me, "What is it with you, Harold? What do you want? You don't even want to go home if you're getting into a fight right before you see the board." I guess the doc was right—the board hit me with a year. And then I went to see them again, and I figured I might be going home this time, and they gave me eighteen months RO—meaning, "reconsideration on." I was mad. I did a year, and I figured maybe the chances were that I would go home. I never figured a year and a half more. So after the eighteen months, I went back again to the parole board, and I didn't know what the hell I was going to get, and they said, "Do you think you are ready to go? We're afraid that you're going to give us a black mark. We don't know what you're going to do out there." I said, "I'll tell you guys the truth. I was ready to go the last time. I felt that then, and I don't feel that I belong here now, and I'm ready to go." They said, "Parole will be in two weeks or a month." Wow! Was I ever happy! They could have given me six months or another year! You never know what they are going to do. They fool you around, and I wasn't expecting to go home. But I was being released! I was going home...again!

DR. SAM: Harold had done his best to sabotage his parole the first time. As he reflects into the tape recorder years later, he understands, in part, his motivation for doing so.

HAROLD: I'll tell you, though, in a way, you don't want to go home because you've made such good friends after five years in prison. But you really do wanna go home, and yet you're nervous about how it's going to be. The change, you know. You can't sleep, you're excited and scared—the responsibility, facing parole, and the whole thing out there of making new friends...and a new life.

DR. SAM: Harold's prison friends threw him a party and gave him a Zippo lighter as a going-away present. Along with the date of his release, they had inscribed on it, "To Harold from the boys," all beautifully etched by hand with a nail. Harold cherished it as "a really great gift that made me feel proud. It really made me feel good that they threw me a party."

Harold was saying goodbye to what had become his surrogate family—a family whom he had become closer to than to his natural one. And, again, there were legitimate reasons for his feeling nervous about going home. During his five years at Sing Sing and Auburn

prisons, his mother never once visited him; his favorite
sister, Elena, visited him one time; and his older brother,
Steven, maybe twice, although he would send him a
package after making a big score. Only Theodore visited
Harold "many, many times," usually when recuperating
in between boxing matches, which Harold and his fellow inmates enjoyed listening to on the prison radio,
making bets on how many rounds the match would go
and whether Theodore would win or lose the fight.

Now it would be Harold who would find himself
in the fight of his life—a fight for normalcy, for rest, for
healing and health. He had all the best intentions.

HAROLD: I landed back on Tenth Street. It was strange walking in the old neighborhood, you know, getting read-
justed with my old friends, living at home again with
Steven. I was scared, nervous. I was trying to go straight.
I got a job in construction. I would work then come
right home and watch TV and eat ice cream, usually a
pint, sometimes a quart. I didn't want to fool around
anymore. I really wanted to go straight in my heart.

So my brother Steven calls me up one night, and
he says, "Hey, do you wanna go to the Latin Quarter?
You wanna hang out and dance?" I said, "No, I don't
want to. I got to get up early and go to work." He says,
"Come on. We'll make some money. We're going to
go out bouncing, me and Stavtros [a former inmate of
Harold's], then we're goin' out drinkin' at a couple of
restaurants the back to the Latin Quarter." I wanted to
stay home, but they finally talked me into it, and I said,
"Okay, I'll meet you at the Latin Quarter."

DR. SAM: That may have been the most consequential *okay*
Harold would ever say in his life. Pictures of him,
Steven, and Stavros were taken by the ladies of the Latin

Quarter; and those pictures found their way into the hands of the police who had been tailing "big criminal" Stavros for some time. Harold had not only violated his probation by being out past curfew but had also violated it by going out to a nightclub! These violations would cost him two years. He made a brief pit stop at Sing Sing before returning to Auburn Prison where he was reunited with Stavros. Ironically, Stavros was sentenced to only one year. In the meantime, Steven was taking it easy back on Tenth Street.

Harold spent little time lamenting his actions. One could even ask if they were subliminally purposeful.

HAROLD: When I went back, it wasn't so hard. I already had five years under my belt. I knew everybody. I was an old-timer. I was accepted in prison. I knew the routine, and I fit right back in like it was an old home. I went right back to the ditch gang and right back to the weights, and it was like I never left. I didn't bother with Stavros but hung out with the same old friends. I was gone a year, but right away it was, "Welcome back, Harold."

DR. SAM: Again, Harold had exchanged one dysfunctional home for another. In many ways, he preferred the supervised routine of prison life to the unsupervised life of Tenth Street. But any sense of well-being would be short-lived.

HAROLD: What happened is, I got in an argument with a guy on the ditch gang. We had a fight, and I had my left ear bit off, the top of my left ear. I ended up going to the hospital to fix it up, and they were afraid that I was going to sue them or something, so they sent me down to Sing Sing for ear operations. I liked Sing Sing 'cause it was big and open, and there was less tension than at Auburn.

I went down there for more operations, and I started hanging out. They were having trouble with an Irish mob down there. They were afraid that there was going to be a war in the prison between the Irish Mob and the Italian Mob, and there might have been. Next thing I know, there was a strike in the prison, and without going into all the details, I was elected to be one of the leaders of the strike! Me and this guy called Ted were the leaders of B block, and I think it lasted two and a half or three days. It was all over TV, and we made demands, and we had the run of the block so that no hacks were allowed.

I was scared because I made demands for the men, and, my God, if I betrayed them or if I made any mistakes, they would have knifed me to death. But I enjoyed being in that position of influence, I guess, as a strike leader over the hacks, plus I had all these men cheering me on. It was nice to be up front, even though I was really scared every morning. But we did it without violence. We had a sit-in strike and we did it without violence, and we won!

DR. SAM: Whether it was fear of reprisals over the "ear incident," a quiet admiration for the way Harold conducted himself during the sit-in, or exhaustion from having to deal with his mercurial nature (or regret for their two-year sentencing), within weeks after the strike, the Parole Board told Harold, "We're throwing you out, Harold. No reprisals. We're letting you go."

HAROLD: "Oh thank God," I shouted! I was on my way home the second time! I was released from Sing Sing on December 7th. I remember 'cause it was Pearl Harbor Day. So now, after doing nearly seven years in prison, with a year in between years 5 and 6, I'm on my way back to Tenth Street, still on parole, and would soon be hanging out with my friends on the street. But I knew, this time, that I never wanted to go back to prison, and I prayed that I never would.

DR. SAM: In spite of being released from Sing Sing on a somewhat heroic note, the odds of Harold never returning were not in his favor. Nor are they today. A US Department of Justice 2018 report estimates that 68 percent of released prisoners were arrested within three years, 79 percent within six years, and 83 percent within nine years. These are staggering statistics, unparalleled in the Western world. We have the highest rate of incarceration. We have the highest rate of recidivism. Could this cycle be broken for Harold? And even if it were, would he be capable of ever fully integrating back into society? What pain would Harold have yet to travel through to find a major breakthrough and substantial healing? Or is Harold's healing beyond human reach, and will it take some form of a miracle to restore him to health and wholeness?

Bellevue Hospital Gate

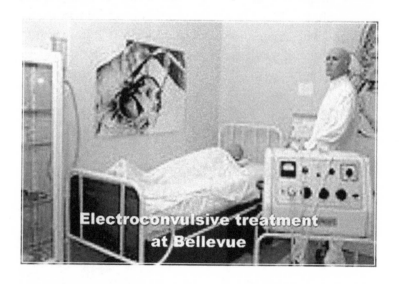

Electroconvulsive treatment at Bellevue

Sing Sing–the country club on the Hudson

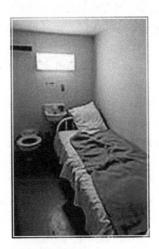

Typical Cell in Sing Sing

Chapter 7

Toxic Soulmates

The dance of death is always a duet.

DR. SAM: Once again, Harold went right back to Tenth Street after leaving prison, and, true to his word, he determined to "go straight" and "never go back to prison." And then he met Maria, and Harold's life would never be quite the same.

HAROLD: I was home only a couple of weeks, and I met this guy Harry Edwards. I knew him when I came out the first time, but just casually. He was a neighbor, and he used to hang out with my brother and with all kinds of Mafioso guys. And what happens is, he says, "Hey, Harold, do you know a girl named Maria?" I said, "I don't know anyone named Maria," and he said, "Yes, you do. She works in the dance hall." I said, "I don't know any girl that works in the dance hall." He says, "She always asks about you, and she says she knows you." I said, "I don't know this girl. Is she pretty?" He says, "Yeah, she's pretty. She has a real nice body, and she knows you."

Naturally, I was curious. So New Year's Eve night, I go up to the dance hall, the old Majestic Dance Hall on Forty-Second Street and Broadway, and I see this pretty blonde and I walk over. She says, "Come on and sit down." I sit down, and I'm talking to her, and I find out that she's Stavros's brother's wife. Stavros's brother's name is Luke, and it was Luke's wife, Maria, whom I had met briefly in Brooklyn when I was home on parole the first time. I says to her, "Why are you telling people that you want to see me? What do you want to see me for? I don't even know you." She says, "Well, I wanted to talk to you," and this and that. I felt uncomfortable, but she says, "You know about me and Luke?" I says, "Yeah, you're married to Luke!"

You see, I was brought up that you never bothered anybody else's wife. You just didn't do things like that. You got hurt for doing things like that. It was against the underworld code, and everyone kept the underworld code. She said, "No, we're separated, and he's living with another woman, and he has a kid by her." I said, "Yeah, but you're still married to him." I didn't want to bother with her. She was my friend's brother's wife.

DR. SAM: Harold had all the best intentions in the world when he returned home from prison. His initial code of conduct with Maria was honorable, and, wisely, he had set up some personal boundaries that he hoped would help keep him from any further involvement with the criminal elements in his neighborhood.

HAROLD: When I came home, I made a decision that I would not bother with Stavros. I didn't want to get involved anymore after that violation of parole with anybody that I knew from prison. In fact, when this guy Arty came out of prison, he looked me up and kept calling and calling the house, and I wouldn't acknowledge his phone calls. I just didn't want to get involved. And I didn't go to Brooklyn to see Stavros. I never looked him up. When guys looked me up, I just told my mother to tell them I wasn't home. Sometimes I would make appointments, but I wouldn't keep them 'cause I didn't want to bother with anyone from prison.

DR. SAM: What Harold didn't know at the time was that some "racket guys" from his neighborhood owned a piece of the Majestic Dance Hall where Maria worked, and the mafiosi would hang around a little bar in front of the dance hall, keeping their eyes on the clientele. One of the racket guys from his neighborhood intro- duced Harold to the other Mafia guys, reassuring them all, "Hey, he just got out. He's just out, and he's a good kid." Being an ex-con allowed Harold to pass muster with the Mafia fraternity, but that acceptance would soon be threatened.

HAROLD: So what happened is that one of the Mafia guys liked Maria, and he was jealous because I was talking to her. Next thing I know, he smacked her and I got up and said, "What are you smacking her for? Are you jealous because she's talking to me?" And then there was this big argument, and I said, "Hey, I'm gonna break someone's head here, I'm gonna break someone's head!" And then he left her and me alone, and I got out of there real quick and tried to forgot about the whole thing. But then Maria got my phone number, looked it up in the telephone book and started calling me. I said, "Look, I can't see you. I don't want to bother with you." Anyway, she kept persistently calling me and calling me. "Please, see me and talk to me," so I met her on a date and told her again, "Listen, you're married to Luke," but she was really pretty, and I was flattered. This girl was calling me. It made me feel good, you know, but I really didn't want to get involved. I was scared, but she kept seducing me, saying, "Aw, Harold, come on, come on."

DR. SAM: Regardless of Harold's desire to go straight, he once again put himself in a vulnerable situation by challenging the Mafia underworld and by seeking intimacy in a relationship that he instinctively knew to be essentially unhealthy. Ironically, Maria's father was a police officer, yet as a "dance hall gal" for hire in a Mafia-owned club, she was in constant contact with the criminal underbelly of New York City. And so began Harold's love-hate relationship with Maria.

HAROLD: I had nothing but a kind of inner contempt for women that worked at dance halls or for bar maids and prostitutes. I put them all in the same category. I just wanted to use them and abuse them, treat them with contempt. And yet, I was attracted to them—to women that were cheap looking, women of the street, women that weren't respected, prostitutes, and things like that. But a decent woman—like a churchgoing woman or just a nice, decent woman, or a mother with children, or a decent neighborhood woman—I wasn't attracted to them. I wasn't worthy of them. They were too high class for me. They were beyond my means.

I don't think I've ever told you this, Dr. Sam, but I once called up Dr. Joyce Brothers, the famous psychologist, on a radio program. I told her all about me, the truth, but I didn't tell her my name. She said I had a classic Madonna-oppressive complex, whatever that means. I knew that I had these things, and I liked to treat woman cruel—dominate them—and yet, I wanted to be babied in some way. I wanted to be dependent upon them. I wanted to be fed. I wanted to be clothed. I wanted to be loved by someone. And I wanted someone I could love.

DR. SAM: At the onset of his relationship with Maria, Harold saw the toxicity in her marriage to his friend's brother and in her criminal connections with the Mafia down at the Majestic Dance Hall. He transparently discloses his own toxicity in the conflicted need to abuse that type of woman, concurrent with his own dependency needs for being loved and cared for. In reaching out to the radio therapist Dr. Joyce Brothers, Harold again shows his desire to understand these conflicted feelings and the subsequent behavior that ensues.

HAROLD: Anyway, I went to bed with Maria on the second date, and, of course, I didn't enjoy it...but I did enjoy it. When I came out of prison the first time, I just went with a couple of prostitutes. But this was different, you know. When I got up the next morning, I decided I wanted to see Maria more often. And the more we saw each other, the more our relationship got better. I started like getting used to her body next to me—having a woman next to me—it really felt strange. All these years I slept alone, all my life, and now a woman would lay in bed next to me. I was fascinated, and she was so very pretty.

DR. SAM: After the sexual abuse by older males in the orphanage, the chronic mistreatment by his female caregivers, and his subsequent chaotic behavior in the community (including random sexual encounters with both women *and* men)—Harold was longing to enter a relationship that met his basic need for true intimacy and one that might stabilize his sometimes confused sexual identity. With Maria, for the first time in his life, Harold was experiencing the positive elements of a more normal relationship with a woman who seemed to like and accept him for who he was. Even so, the spiritual values planted in him while attending the orphanage Sunday School prompted his rightful concern about cheating and committing adultery.

HAROLD: On that first night I went to be with Maria, it was like cheating, of course. I was committing adultery, and I didn't enjoy it. But I did enjoy it. It's like the Bible says, "The pleasures of sin for a season." So the months went by, and we had an affair. She would get through work at four in the morning, and I would meet her, and we would stay all night and sometimes stay two days together. And I felt guilty because she was a married woman, and even though she was separated from her husband, I still knew the guy! I had all these guilty feelings, and every time we would meet, it was like we would sneak. It was like I was hiding from somebody that might see me, and yet, I loved her. It was like I was hooked on her, and she was hooked on me, dominating me. She would give me money, and then I'd pay for everything—dinner, beer, cigarettes—but she was the one in control, and I felt I was always sucking off of her.

I'd make her pay for the hotel when we'd spend the night together! I'd pay for it at the front desk, but she'd have given me the money! I don't know, it was like I was a pimp or somethin', and somehow it made me feel like I was in control. And she loved it and could be kind and gentle with me and would feed me. And I wanted to be fed. It made me feel wanted. It made me feel loved. It made me feel more special than anybody else, and it made me feel…sexually excited.

But you know, Dr. Sam, I had no real respect for her or myself. I felt contempt for any woman that I automatically went to bed with. I thought if a woman went to bed with someone, that meant she was no good. And though I was hooked on Maria and loved her, I had this contempt for her. I guess it was all sort of masochistic. I don't know.

DR. SAM: A psychologist, whom Harold was seeing at the time, had counseled him to pull away from what had become an unhealthy, enabling relationship. Guilt, secrecy, domination, control, and contempt are hardly the stepping-stones to a solid and loving relationship. But Harold's need to feel wanted, loved, and special was stronger than the guilt and contempt he felt for himself and Maria. The peculiarities of love are endless, and even a semblance of it will "satisfy for a season," as Harold so aptly noted.

It would take a chance encounter with an old prison acquaintance for Harold to put an end to the relationship.

HAROLD: I used to meet Maria after the dance hall closed, like four in the morning, and I'm waiting for her to come out one night, when a Cadillac pulls up. And who is in the Cadillac but an old friend of mine, Sandor. Sandor's in the car with another guy called Jackie. Now Sandor is a Mafia guy, and he's from my neighborhood. In fact, I did time with him in Sing Sing, and he's in the car sitting on the right-hand side and Jackie is behind the wheel. And guess who's in the middle? Maria's in the middle! My gal is sittin' in the middle between two guys!

So I walk over to the car and I say, "Hi, Sandor. How ya doin? Hi, Jackie." Sandor says, "Hi, Harold."

I said, "Hey, who's the pretty girl?" He says, "I'll introduce you. This is Maria." I said, "Hello, Maria," and she just looked at me, didn't say nothin'. She just looked at me! I said to myself, "————! My gal is in this car with these racket guys!" And I just turned around and went home and told myself I'm not gonna bother with her no more!

So anyway, we stopped going together, but then she calls me up and she says, "I'll never see them again! I promise you, Harold, I'll never see them again!" Well, I was feelin' tinges of jealousy and anger and feelin' this was not going to go anyplace good, and I thought for sure I wasn't going to see her, but then I ended up seeing her—and I kept seeing her over and over—it was like I was developing an addiction.

DR. SAM: Following neither his therapist's advice nor his own better instincts, Harold had reengaged with Maria more obsessively than ever. We frequently receive love wherever we can find it, never asking ourselves the important questions that need to accompany a commitment to another person. During their stormy, passionate affair, Harold and Maria never paused to ask themselves those questions: Other than the immediacy of a strong sexual attraction, what things do we have in common to sustain a long-term relationship? Is there a deep trustworthiness in the relationship that can be counted on consistently by both parties? Is there a mutual respect for the total person? Is our love exploitative, only interested in meeting our immediate, subjective needs?

HAROLD: Then all of a sudden, she was in a hurry to get married! I'd already told her to get a divorce; otherwise, I wouldn't see her anymore. And she did, she got a divorce, and I think it was now that her ex, Luke, was getting married to the girl that he had a baby with, and I think she wanted to beat Luke to it or to feel she wasn't left out or to get revenge on him with me. I don't know what her motives were, but she was making a deadline fast, saying, "We ought to get married, Harold!"

I didn't want to get married to her, Dr. Sam. I didn't trust her. I had no confidence in her. But I was in love. It was like I was hooked on her. She threatened to withdraw sex and never see me again if I didn't marry her. So we stopped sneaking around, and I ended up finally marrying Maria.

DR. SAM: The marriage would not get off to an auspicious start. While on their honeymoon, Harold was moonlighting as a bouncer at a bar called Reno's. His brother-in-law (Elena's husband Otis) owned it. One night, Harold had to subdue a drunken sailor and ended up breaking his own leg in the altercation. While recuperating, Maria put up the money for an apartment on Thirty-Fourth Street, allowing them to setup a home together. Any dream of conjugal bliss was short-lived.

HAROLD: Now that I was married, I really wanted to take the man's role. I treated her differently. After I married Maria, it was like she was a good woman now, and I didn't want her to work at the Majestic anymore. She was my wife now, and I really opened up to her. I let my hair down and showed her my heart and tried to let her in. This tough guy... I could show emotion now, but she didn't respond positively to that. She responded negatively.

When I was going out with her, she was content. Now, I became like a creep to her, like the guys she had contempt for down at the dance hall. Now she was asking me for money, and I became like a John to her. Give me, take me, buy me! But I still enjoyed sex with her, but then after a while, she started denying me that! She continued to work in the dance hall, and I continued to try and change her. I'd tell her to stop working there. But subconsciously, somewhere I still wanted to be fed by her. I felt like I was doing the feeding now. She was sucking from me emotionally in some kind of way. I don't know what it was, but my needs were not being met. I was like screaming inside, and Maria...she just grew more and more distant emotionally, then would come back for a little while, and then would leave me emotionally again.

DR. SAM: As so often happens in relationships that lack a secure multidimensional foundation, a "dance of death" had begun even before the wedding orchestra had played its first tune. Harold was once again feeling emotionally abandoned, yet he was incapable of extricating himself from the very relationship that was causing his pain. Harold and Maria—they had indeed become toxic soulmates.

Chapter 8

Harold's Obsession

Obsession is like being on a treadmill and never getting off.

DR. SAM: Pulitzer Prize-winning American novelist Norman Mailer was married six times and convicted of assault for stabbing his second wife, Adele Morales, nearly killing her. Not surprisingly, nine years later, Mailer ran for mayor of New York City—it's a crazy town.

Though not as overtly violent as Mailer, Harold would wrestle over and over with the same questions he couldn't answer: Why does Maria keep leaving me? Why does she come back to me when she says she doesn't want to be with me anymore? Why does she taunt me sexually? Is she being unfaithful? How can I earn her respect again? And, of course, the penultimate question that every frustrated lover/partner/ spouse asks him or herself, Why doesn't she/he love me anymore? And when that question is followed with "Or maybe she/he really does love me," then you know that the relentless mental treadmill of obsession has taken hold.

HAROLD: I'd just got back from visiting my sister and nephews in Georgia, and there was something wrong between us when I returned. I loved her, but I knew something was wrong. In my heart, I said, "Something has happened," and I didn't know what it was. I just sensed it. It was not the same. She was acting different, and I sensed it.

Later that night while we were talking, she said, "You know, while you were away, Alex drove me home one night. [Alex V was the owner of the Majestic Dance Hall.] He drove me home from the dance hall, and he came up, and we had coffee." I said, "Why's he coming up here? He shouldn't be here at my house while I'm away. How dare he!" I looked at her, and I could sense the guilt. She was real, real quiet. Then she said, "Nothing happened." When she told me this, I really felt that she was trying to tell me something, like she wanted to acknowledge something. I knew... I knew... she couldn't come right out and tell me, but it was her way of telling me that while I was away, she had had intercourse with Alex V.

I had been rejected, and I felt like I was being abandoned. I was hurt. I didn't know how to handle it. I became angry. I went into the other room and punched the hell out of the wall and yelled, "I'm going to kill that ———! I'm going to kill him!" Maria was crying in the other room, and I knew. I just knew she had sex with him while I was gone, and I hated him. I was jealous, I was furious, and [I] didn't know how to handle it.

Dr. Sam, it really bothers me that there's a world where guys like this can really mess a marriage up. But who am I to judge, I suppose. I mean, look at the things that I've done. But I gotta tell you, things were never, never the same.

Dr. Sam: When trust is shattered, it's very difficult to rebuild a broken relationship. It matters not the social stratum;

few couples possess the commitment to honesty and forgiveness which healing requires. Restoration is possible, but infidelity is a formidable hurdle. There is a reason that Moses and Jesus address the issue of adultery in the Bible: they're not trying to be killjoys; quite the opposite, they know that adultery destroys families and lives. Their admonition and hope are that the pain of betrayal, separation, and divorce might be avoided.

But the truth is, both Harold and Maria would be unfaithful multiple times. They came into their relationship from emotionally fractured families. Both Maria's father and mother were alcoholics, so in her own way, Maria was as emotionally abused as Harold. Prompted by Harold's inability to forgive, adjust, and cope, Maria would soon be on the run. And Harold would soon be chasing after her.

HAROLD: At this time my mother-in-law, Maria's mother, moved into our house on Thirty-Fourth Street and stayed three or four weeks, and Maria didn't want to have sex at night when her mom was there, and we got in an argument over it. Finally I said, "I'm going to leave if she doesn't leave," and I moved out and waited for three or four days. When I came back, there was no apartment. Everything was gone. Maria was gone. She had gone to Brooklyn to live with her sister, and I started running after her like crazy, trying to get back together with her. But there was nothing happening. She'd talk, but when it came time like to get together, there was always an excuse. The message was clear: "I don't love you. I'm cheating on you with someone else." It was infuriating me. I was running after her, and the more she was running away from me, the more frustrated I became and the more I was running after her.

What I really was afraid of was that she had abandoned me completely.

DR. SAM: Emotionally, Harold was like that little four-year-old boy left on the front lawn of the orphanage: "I was really so scared—just a scared little boy. I tell ya, I just felt so forlorn." And like many others who have experienced abusive trauma as children, Harold's thoughts and emotions were fixated on having an intimate, loving relationship with Maria; so fixated that he became obsessed with her, transitioning from a normal, volitional preoccupation of her to an uncontrollable, manic fixation. Time and again, he compulsively said and did things that inevitably resulted in further anxiety and pain, all repetitious of his earlier, childhood experiences. Yet Harold was powerless to resist.

HAROLD: I used to call her up all the time—sometimes three or four times a night. "I want to see you!" I'd say, but she always would give me an excuse, "I got to go to work" or "I got to go here. I've got an appointment." I'd go down to see her at the dance hall and she'd just ignore me, and it would infuriate me. It was getting so that I couldn't function at work [Reno's Bar]. My mind was in a fog, always on her like a broken record. I felt like crying all the time. I felt like an electric wire, like, "Zzzzzzzzz," this tension, depression—this tremendous pressure all the time.

I wanted to be free, but I wasn't. I wanted to be fed, but I didn't want to be fed in the sick way like before. Maria was my wife, but she was treating me with contempt like I used to treat her. And I still wanted to be babied. I still wanted to be fed. Yet I didn't, and I felt like I was going nuts, and my mind would just keep going on and on about her.

Otis, my brother-in-law, finally said, "If you can't do your job, Harold, you'll have to get out." That just gave me more fear. If I lose my job, then what? It was all just driving me crazy, and I was afraid I was going to have a total crack-up.

DR. SAM: Even as when he was in Sing Sing, Harold's greatest fear was that he would have a complete crack-up. Now he was imprisoned by his obsessive mind, unable to see the different results he wished for and confused by the complexity of his own needs. His emotional stress and depression were being internally amplified and reaching unbearable levels; so much so that Harold began to lose control and felt he was going crazy.

Obsessive-compulsive behavior can have temporary stress relief, but then it has to be repeated over and over, driven by a negative energy that seeks release. Harold was increasingly unable to function as his mind continued to be "electric" with constant thoughts of Maria. Now, when those irrational thoughts and fears triggered compulsive behavior, there would be no satisfaction nor respite from his obsession.

HAROLD: So what happened is, Christmas came, and I got off from work early, and I went down to the dance hall, and I bought flowers for her and rented a hotel room so that she would have no excuse. I told her after she got through at four thirty in the morning that I would take her out to dinner and after we could go up to the hotel that was right near Times Square where she worked. So I gave her the flowers right after work, and she was holding them, and she looked at me and said, "Why don't you give them to your mother?" She was, like, telling me, "Screw you, I don't want them." She was walking with a girlfriend, and she was so...scornful that

I didn't have a place of my own and that I was living at my mother's house. "Don't you have to go back to your mother's house, Harold? You're living over at your mother's house, aren't you? A momma's boy! Harold's a momma's boy!"

I shouted back, "Leave! Get the hell out of here!" but I really didn't want her to go. And when she and her girlfriend walked away, my heart broke. I just started crying and felt completely defeated. I thought, "I can't take this. I can't take this running around after her, and I can't take her rejecting me. I don't know what's going on." But I kept crying and called my brother and said, "Steven, please come and get me. I'm sick. Please come and get me," and I told him where I was. He came up in a car, and I got in and he just looked at me for the longest time. Finally, I said, "I can't take it anymore," and I cried like a baby. He took me home to my mother's house, and I knew it was the end really, but I still didn't want to give up. I started to chase her and run after her, and I was hopelessly hooked, just like I was hooked on a drug. All I could think about was her and how I wanted to be in her presence. I wanted her and yet was repelled at the same time. It just was crazy, Dr. Sam, because it went on and on.

DR. SAM: Feeling desperate, Harold went against his better instincts to win Maria back and ended up doing a stickup downtown—a truck hijacking with a couple of guys from the old neighborhood. Rather than accept the end of his relationship, he took the default position of fighting back, which he'd been groomed for from his combative days in the orphanage. Harold would do whatever was necessary to keep Maria.

HAROLD: I went in on the stickup job so that I could get some money for a place where we could live. Then I could say, "Look, Maria, I got an apartment!" She had said to me one day, "I'll go back with you, Harold, if we have an apartment." She said the reason she wasn't with me and wouldn't come back was because I didn't have an apartment. I didn't have the money, and she knew it, so I did the job. It was probably a lot of ———— on her part. If I had gotten that apartment, she probably wouldn't have come back anyway.

I know it was perverse, Dr. Sam, but I wanted Maria back more than ever. But now I wanted to get her back for a different reason. I wanted to have dominance over her. I wanted to have her beg for forgiveness. It was pride. It was ego. I lived on this hate. I wanted her back to break her, hear her beg for mercy, and say "I'm sorry." And I didn't know how to stop this hate. I felt I was in a battle, my arms and teeth were clinched, and my will was set in stone.

DR. SAM: Apartment or no apartment, Maria, in all probability, wouldn't have gone back to Harold permanently. But she did open the door sufficiently for him to reenter her life. Harold was released on bail for the truck hijacking and inexplicably never convicted of the crime. Maria, seemingly flattered by Harold's wanting to provide for her, took an active, if not morbid, interest in the case (perhaps with the help of her policeman father?) and made intermittent attempts to reconcile with Harold during this period.

To some degree, she was helping keep "the dance of death" alive, giving Harold just enough encouragement to energize his obsession. But was Maria to blame for Harold's manic behavior? No. If she *hadn't* opened the door, he would have *broken* it down. And Maria instinctively knew that. With his "arms and teeth clinched," Harold was not yet at the breaking point where he could let go, set aside his will, and surrender his obsession for Maria and the old life he had known for so long. That "breaking point" crucible was critical to Harold's healing, but it wouldn't come without "help" from an old Mafia acquaintance.

Chapter 9

The Broken Code

"Wise guys" enforce their code of ethics with fear.

Dr. Sam: Whether in prison or in the old neighborhood, the Mafia was a ubiquitous presence in Harold's life. It was like a menacing dark shadow, malevolently permeating his psyche. In many ways, the Mafia was the "shadow" civil authority of the streets and of the prisons. They remain so today, with a recent renaissance in their pervasive influence. Though Harold admired these wise guys from a distance, he had done little to ingratiate himself into their good graces. His relationship with Maria and her friends down at the Majestic Dance Hall put him in precarious proximity to the Mafia kingpins of Manhattan, including Johnny Dio who did "dirty work" for Jimmy Hoffa and was indicted for planning an acid attack on newspaper columnist Victor Riesel, which left him blind. But innocently enough, it would be a chance meeting at a charitable street festival that would send Harold careening off the tracks and headed directly toward that dreaded crack-up.

HAROLD: So what happens is, I go to this Italian Street Festival, and at one of the gambling concessions, there is this guy there by the name of Jason T who hangs out down at the dance hall. He's a member of the Mafia, and he's known to have killed at least three or four guys. It was common knowledge in my neighborhood.

He was older and like a captain in the Mafia— something like that—and I go over by his concession stand, and he sees me and says, "Hi, Harold, do you want to play the game?" and I says, "No, I don't want to play." Next thing I know, he says, "How's Maria?" and I says, "She's okay." I didn't want to give him any information. He was a guy that I never trusted 'cause Maria had told me he had the hots for her and was always looking to make moves on her, and she always thought that he was a creep and didn't want to bother with him. Anyway, so then he says, "But you're not married to Maria anymore." I said, "What do you mean? We're just separated. I'm still married to her." He says, "No, you ain't married." I said, "I am married. Don't tell me that I'm not married." I started getting angry that he would even question me. My marriage was none of his business!

Next thing I know, he says, "You know it's all over Broadway, Harold, that Alex V and Maria are having an affair." I says, "What?" He says, "Not only that, but me and Peter B [another Mafia guy] followed her, and they went to a hotel together." And he keeps tellin' me over and over that they're having this affair and everybody knows it! I was goin' crazy inside! Then he says to me, "He deserves to get his ——— head blown off." He was telling me, "Hey, Harold, you should kill Alex V. Shoot him in the head!" He was ratting on and setting up his own best friend of twenty years and wanting me to kill him!

DR. SAM: What Harold didn't know at the time was that he too was being set up. Jason T was lending money to prop up Alex V as the titular owner of the Majestic. Jason figured that with Alex out of the way, he could take over the entire dance hall operation. And with Harold arrested for murder (or killed by the Mafia for killing Alex!), Maria would have no option but to run to him—her boss and protectorate. The question is, would Harold take the bait?

HAROLD: I felt I was exposed. I felt I was raped. "You're not a man but a cuckold," I feared they would say. And in my neighborhood, if you were cuckolded and knew who did it to you, you had to kill him. If you didn't kill him, you were a punk. I became, like, crazy, Dr. Sam. I didn't know what to do but would still do anything to avoid Maria leaving me and breaking the marriage up. And yet I knew it was like an impossible situation. How crazy was that? I can't get her back but gotta have her.

So one night, I get drunk with a friend. I was bombed. It was like I wanted to commit suicide drinking. I lined the shots on the bar, and I knocked them down, one after another. I said to my friend, "Drive me to Brooklyn." He said, "I don't want to drive you to Brooklyn," but he did drive me all the way and let me off by Maria's house. It was like two or three in the morning, and I went upstairs, and I had this birthday card in my hand. It was Maria's birthday, and I thought the card was like a token of love, and I was listening by the door, and I heard her and her sister talking, and I was just so crazy. I was like a doormat. I laid on the floor, and I pushed the card under the door, and I was going to walk away, but I was drunk. I was bombed, and I was on my knees, and I was pushing this card under the door, so then I figured I would walk away. And in my drunken stupor, I figured she would see it, and she did and said somethin' like, "What's that underneath the door?" And then she opened the door, and there I am lying down on my face, and she looked at me and said, "Harold. I have no respect for you!" and threw the card at me and slammed the door in my face!

This really killed me, Dr. Sam, because I knew it was all over. Our marriage was all over. I didn't know how I was going to live without her, and I went crazy and broke down the door. She had locked herself in the bedroom and wouldn't come out. Her sister and her niece was there in the living room, but Maria wouldn't come out of the bedroom where, unbeknownst to me, she was calling the cops. Like it seemed only a couple of minutes and two squad cars came, and then she came out of the bedroom and said, "I want him out of here. I don't want him in this house! We're separated, and he's always sneaking around after me, and plus"—and when she said this, it really killed me—"he's an ex-con!"

The cops say, "Come on, buddy, leave," and I started to resist them. I was so mad and said, "Don't put your hands on me!" But I went with them, and it was the last time I ever saw Maria! When I walked out the door, she looked at me with a smile like a Cheshire cat. I was so hurt, and she knew it…callin' me an ex-con. The cops could have thrown the book at me. I went downstairs, and one cop said to me, "Hey, buddy. You don't want to go back to that house. You don't want to go back to that woman. You're better off not there." They were right. But it broke my heart, and I wept like crazy.

DR. SAM: Of this we can be certain—there is no justification for Harold's behavior. Tragically, the abused child had become the abusive man. Though Harold's defense might be "I never laid a hand on her," the psychic abuse was poisonous. Maria represents millions of women who have been badgered and battered psychologically by the relentless, abusive behavior of a lover or spouse.

When the police came to her Brooklyn apartment and Maria identified Harold as an ex-con, he lashed out in self-justification: "You tell them that I'm an ex-con, and you tell them that I come around here sneaking, but you don't tell them that you have been cheating on me all this time!" Harold failed to recognize that he alone was responsible for his behavior. Tragically, we are witnessing in this country a rise of abuse. From the Hollywood Hills to Harvard Square, there remain too many men who will justify their abusive actions by accusing the injured party of having precipitated those actions, thus absolving themselves of all accountability.

To paraphrase Shakespeare, it would take Harold years to realize that the fault was not in Maria, but rather, the fault was in him. He, and he alone, had to take responsibility.

Years later, as I listened to Harold whisper his intimate thoughts into the tape recorder, it became evident that he had come to a broader understanding of himself and Maria, as indicated by the following mea culpa.

HAROLD: I know I was a very sick guy, Dr. Sam. And it's funny, but I don't blame Maria now. I was a momma's boy. I was dependent, I was wounded, and I was very sick. I broke her down with my hate. I condemned her. I even called her a prostitute. I said that it was her fault that I was sick. I admit to all these things…and so much more.

DR. SAM: This recognition, a prerequisite to healing, would come painstakingly, and to quote the Psalmist, Harold would have to "walk through the valley of the shadow of death" before healing could take place.

HAROLD: The next few weeks were like a complete disoriented fog, yet I knew the moment I went over the wire. I was walking down St. Mark's Place, and I was confused, losing weight, my mind in a fog, when all of a sudden, I realized that I had been set up to be killed. They were setting me up to commit murder, and you know, if I had trouble with them and we argued, they would kill me. You just don't do things like that. You don't go telling a guy your wife is cheating on you. You don't look to set him up for murder and then have him murdered. But that's what Jason T was doing…that's what they wanted to do to me!

And then, as if to prove it, I bump into Johnny Dio one night at a restaurant. As I was leaving, he yells out after me, "Take care of yourself, Harold, and make sure you don't get hit by a truck." In that instant, I felt like my whole world crashed! The whole underworld code that I built my life on—trust between friends, never ratting—they broke that code. And even though I never had any dealings with these guys—they were like heroes, I looked up to them, the Mafia—and it was like everything I had built upon was built on sand, and I had nothing left.

My secret was out. I wasn't really a man. I was a punk, a girl. Jason T had raped me psychologically, and I felt castrated and everybody knew it—everybody on Broadway knew it, everybody in my neighborhood knew it! Maria had left me for Alex V and was no longer my wife, and I felt castrated by her and my so-called friends. I had nothing left to live for.

DR. SAM: It seemed as if Harold had hit rock bottom. The isolated child had become the isolated adult. And isolation is a perilous space for any of us. Would there be a deus ex machina in Harold's life—a lifeline, a friend, a new moral code of conduct, a transforming faith, a parent, a pastor, or a therapist who would come to the rescue? Or would Harold have to walk through this "valley of the shadow of death" alone?

One of the WiseGuys

Chapter 10

The Crack-Up

The ultimate torture chamber is a tortured mind.

DR. SAM: Bereft of family, "friends," and his wife, Harold would experience an extreme isolation that would leave a deliriant imprint on his mind, eventually manifesting itself in erratic, even hallucinatory behavior.

HAROLD: My whole world was grey. Everything was grey—dull, flat. Everything was lifeless. My life was one big hopeless grey. There was no life, no color. My life was over. I'd be walking down the streets, and the tears would be running down my face. All I did was think about the past. I rehashed it over and over and over. I nursed the grudges and lived on the hate and anger and resentment. I felt like a dog in a square box and there was no way out. It was a square box—up, down, left, right, and all the way around. I was completely trapped and couldn't get out. I was alone.

DR. SAM: Psychologically, Harold's mental isolation was reminiscent of the box in prison and the attic in the orphanage. Only one coping mechanism seemed to assuage the pain, recalling the days when he binged on ice cream to calm his nerves before the anxiety of a heist.

HAROLD: I was eating and eating and eating ravenously. I couldn't stop. It was like I wanted to fill up an empty hole that was in my heart, and I couldn't fill it up. All I used to think about was escaping this tremendous fear and anxiety and pain, so I'd eat sweets and ice cream all day long, like an alcoholic would go to alcohol or a junkie would go to drugs. I went to food. Breakfast was potatoes and cake and candy and ice cream. Eggs sometimes but cakes and ice cream all day long.

Then I started going to therapy again and was put on some pills, valium and different things, and I lost weight rapidly. But it was like I was on a yo-yo-first gaining, then losing, gaining, losing, over and over. Next thing you know, though, in a few months, my clothes were hanging on me and I looked like I just got out of a concentration camp. My eyes were hollow, and I just looked like this sad, tormented man.

DR. SAM: To his credit, Harold had reached out again for help. Even in his mental fog, he had the presence of mind to call up a free clinic, screaming in desperation at the therapist on the other end of the line, "Please help me! I can't take it! You've got to help me! I can't take it anymore!"

Psychologist Dr. Holst did his best to stabilize Harold's emotions and reduce his self-destructive behavior. But even with medication judiciously administered, it was nearly impossible to calm Harold's charged mind.

HAROLD: It...how can I describe it? It felt like it was chewing itself to death. Like my mind was eating on itself. That's it. My mind was eating itself up and being destroyed by its own thoughts. I was in unbelievable torment...

despair…completely hopeless. I was listless, yet at the same time, I had this tremendous anger and rage. I wanted to put my head through the walls, Dr. Sam, so that I could wash my brains out—just wash my brains right out of my head.

DR. SAM: Dr. Holst knew what desperate shape Harold was in. At one point, he uncharacteristically told him, "Your psychological life is at stake. I don't know if you're going to make it or be a living vegetable for the rest of your life." Harold may have been embellishing Dr. Holst's response, but the caring doctor had reason to be alarmed.

HAROLD: I felt that in my heart and head there were like a thousand bees stinging me with hate and hurt all the time. I was in pain and torment constantly. And I had fantasies, all kinds of fantasies, that I lived over and over in my mind. I killed Alex V and I killed Jason T. I murdered them over and over! I wanted to kill them so bad, but I was afraid to because they were Mafia, and if I killed them, I would either go to jail or be killed. It was this thing about murdering and being killed, day and night, over and over in my head. I kept hearing Johnny Dio saying, "Take care of yourself, Harold, and make sure you don't get hit by a truck." So every time I went home at night, I would be looking in cars to see if someone was going to shoot me in the head. I had these fantasies that the Mafia were going to throw me in the crusher (a garbage truck), and I was full of fear. At night, Dr. Sam, I used to hide in the apartment and look out the window for people who were coming to kill me or to castrate me. I was living in this little furnished room all by myself and would lie in my bed all night and fantasize about people coming to kill me.

DR. SAM: As in Harold's case, when the mind receives the same stimuli repeatedly and with such intensity, it can become difficult to distinguish between what is real or imagined. Soon, Harold would be incapable of separating his fantasies from reality. On the tape recorder, one can hear his quivering voice reliving the moment.

HAROLD: I'm in bed...lying there it seemed all night...having all these crazy thoughts that people are going to kill me, and I couldn't take it anymore, Dr. Sam, and I get up and go to the window and start to scream and scream at a car that's coming up the block to get me. I'm just sure they're coming to get me. And a neighbor must have called the cops 'cause the next thing I know, they come in a couple of squad cars and an ambulance and they think that I'm gonna jump...and maybe I was... and I'm screaming at them, "Don't come up here! I'll kill you, you bastards," 'cause in my head I thought they were Mafia guys dressed up as cops.

Next thing you know, they get in somehow and jump me and try to tie me down and handcuff me. They were holding me down, and I thought they were going to rape me. There were six or seven of them in this small room, and they were running into each other and cursing at me as my body stiffened up like a board. And finally they get my hands and legs cuffed and stuff me into this black bag and put me in the ambulance and drive me to Bellevue. When I get there, they cuff me to a rolling bed with metal things on the side, and I was sure they had put me in a room that was a torture chamber.

DR. SAM: It was now officially in the records of Bellevue Hospital, the thing Harold feared the most—a "complete crack-up" had transpired. Bellevue's more clinical classification might have been "schizophrenia with paranoia," but in many ways, Harold defied simple classification and was a composite of several mental and emotional conditions, illnesses which I saw every day in my office and hospital practice in California.

With little outlet for his anger and pain, the next few months *would* be a torture chamber for Harold, as he turned his rage inward and inflicted dreadful, physical abuse upon himself.

As I listened to his cries on the recorder, I couldn't help but reflect on Dr. Holst's concern about Harold ending up a "living vegetable." I didn't share his fatalistic view. I knew hope and healing were possible.

Chapter 11

Words of Kindness

A light touch and kind word defuse many a troubled soul.

DR. SAM: Handcuffed to the hospital bed and feeling like a cornered and tortured animal, the police continued to interrogate Harold until a nurse on duty firmly intervened.

HAROLD: "Leave him alone!" she ordered them. And the next thing I know, she came over to me, this nurse—and I'll never forget this—she put her hand on my back and said, "It's going to be okay, Harold." That's all she said to me while patting me on the back, "It's going to be okay, Harold." She was like some kind of a protector, and she looked at me with such kindness and love, and I really appreciated it. It was some kind of spark that touched me.

Finally, they unshackled me and the cops left, and some orderlies put me in the bathroom and took all my clothes and belongings and put a gown on me. They took me up to a room, a seclusion room, and I was imagining that people were speaking to me in there. But I was only hearing it in my head, so I kept saying the nurse's words over and over, "It's going to be okay, Harold, it's going to be okay."

DR. SAM: In the midst of Harold's mental chaos, one of the healers in his life would be this caring nurse who patted him on the back, called him by name, looked at him with kindness, and spoke those simple six words: "It's going to be okay, Harold." All of us, at one time or another, have needed that pat on the back and those encouraging words. Many of us never would have made it without them.

The spark that touched Harold was the nurse's unconditional acceptance of him in that exposed moment of crisis and those comforting words could have been given only by someone outside Harold's fractured circle of family and friends. Those words triggered a new beginning for Harold, but it was a beginning that would need many more words of kindness along the way from a variety of people. Dr. Holst would play a leading role.

HAROLD: At first, I didn't want to talk to him or to anyone. I remember it was near Christmastime, and the doc asked, "Why don't you draw something, Harold?" I finally drew a little picture—just a stick figure of the arms and legs and face of a small boy—and I drew a word coming out of his mouth, and it said, "Help."

I remember I would just sit there with Dr. Holst, staring, and he was asking me questions, and I was will-less and listless—so completely confused and disoriented that I didn't know what he was talking about. At first, I saw him as cruel and would just sit and stare. Later on, he told me that when I came in for sessions, he'd remove the ashtray and paperweight from his desk because he thought that I was going to throw them at him.

But he stuck with me month after month, and slowly, I began to trust him a little. He wouldn't let me talk about Maria, but I could talk about anything else. I used to tell him, "People are after me, and they're going to kill me, and they're outside the door now." He used to say, "Get up, Harold, and look out the door," and I'd get up and open the door and there'd be no one there. He'd say, "See, no one's there. It's all in your mind. When you have these thoughts, test them out against reality." He was my link with sanity.

DR. SAM: In addition to asking Harold not to talk about Maria, Dr. Holst also suggested that it might be time to consider a divorce. Harold eventually agreed, and several months later, Maria (somewhat reluctantly) signed the divorce papers. Harold was doing the difficult work of beginning a new life.

HAROLD: I knew I was very ill, but something deep inside of me wanted help and wanted life. Dr. Sam, I just have to pause right now to thank you…thank you for helping me…for asking me to do this…speak out all my thoughts. And I want to thank Dr. Holst too because somehow, deep down inside, with his help, I was able to make a decision and say to myself, "I'm not going to let this beat me," 'cause I knew that my very life was at stake.

DR. SAM: Harold was beginning to trust again, not only in Dr. Holst but, more importantly, in himself. When he had first arrived at Bellevue, Harold described himself as "a broken man…walking around with pajamas on, shuffling my feet, taking little baby steps like a timid, frightened, scared man."

Listening to this image, I recalled seeing many persons in the same condition when a few years earlier, I had served a psychology internship at Manteno State Hospital in Illinois. Sadly, many of those patients never recovered from their state of complete brokenness.

But with the care of that kind nurse and the dedicated staff at Bellevue, within a few months, Harold had stabilized and was soon attending group therapy and a variety of social activities, including dance lessons and, of all things, prayer meetings.

HAROLD: A patient there at the hospital, a young lady, started prayer meetings in the evening before bedtime. It was the highlight of my day. I loved gathering around in a circle with other people and praying. I was getting out of myself, and it was like I was reaching out to God, perhaps for the first time since I went to chapel back at the orphanage.

And at these meetings, Dr. Sam, what I was really picking up on was not so much the exact words, but it was like the inflection in people's voices. It hit me very deep down when people spoke kind to me. Like when that nurse patted me on the back when I was handcuffed and said, "You're going to be okay, Harold." When people would talk to me that way—and they had this sort of gentle, loving tone in their voice—that's what I would respond to.

DR. SAM: In the end, isn't that what we all respond to positively—a gentle, loving voice? Fortunately, there would be other gentle and kind people who would make their way to Bellevue Hospital and visit Harold, including his landlady who brought him sweets, along with words of encouragement. Surprisingly, as if a gift from heaven, Harold's mother came up from Virginia to visit him, and other family members soon followed.

HAROLD: Someone got hold of my mother and told her where I was, not right away, but finally they told her and she came to see me! I don't know what it was, Dr. Sam, but her visit seemed to snap me out of something. Then my sister Nora came from Virginia. And then my sister Jena came from Georgia with my nieces. They traveled so far to come and see me. And Elena, sweet Elena, came nearly every day it seemed. Even my nephew Owen came to visit me on Christmas Day. He was such a sweet kid. He gave me a radio to listen to music, and that really helped me. It was like therapeutic. There was only a couple of radios in the whole ward, and guys would come to me and want to listen to music, and it brought people around me and got me out of thinking about myself.

In some strange way, my family had come back to me, and there was something to hold on to again. There was some reality from the outside to hold on to. And I started reading about Jesus and praying, "God, please get me out of here. I'll do anything."

When my mother came and visited me again [she'd moved back to New York], I said, "Ma, please get me out. I want to go home." I saw the psychiatrist, and in about a week or so, I was sent home to live with my mother. I knew then I never wanted to come back.

DR. SAM: Harold continued treatment at Dr. Holst's outpatient office, and eventually, he was able to show his appreciation for the care and support he had received from him during his extensive therapy.

HAROLD: One day during the course of a therapy session, he asked me for a match. Dr. Holst smoked a pipe and cigars, just like Freud, I guess. But I said to myself, "I have matches on me. I smoke, but I'm not going to give him a match. I wouldn't give anybody anything for so long. He was treating me for free all this time, and I wouldn't give him a match to light his pipe! He was always so kind and was really the start of someone loving me just as I was. So one day, months later, as I was leaving his office, I reached in my pocket and took out a book of matches and tore one off and left it on his desk and walked out quickly. That was my way of saying, "I'm reaching out. I want to give you something." The next week, I left him a book of matches, and a month later, at Christmastime, I bought him a pipe lighter. He really loved it. I was saying to someone for the first time in a long time, "I trust you, and I'm going to let you into my heart. And thank you for all your help!" Boy, what a wonderful man he was!

DR. SAM: Harold's will to live had been awakened. The fog—that grey mental landscape that had dominated his mind for years—was lifting. He was starting to see colors again and was taking an interest in "giving back," a sure sign that healing was underway. Harold didn't realize that he was starting, in small ways, to experience the results of following Christ's message: "For whoever wants to save his life will lose it, but whoever loses his life for me and for the gospel will save it" (Mark 8:35, NIV).

Harold wasn't ready to "offer his life as a sacrifice and serve God by serving others" yet, but he would soon take advantage of opportunities opening up for him to "give back."

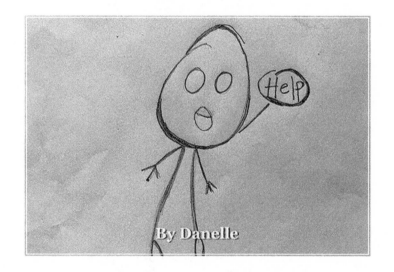

Chapter 12

Simple Steps

Simplicity is a powerful antidote for the anxious spirit.

DR. SAM: Harold's release from Bellevue Hospital would be qualitatively different than when he was released from the orphanage and from Sing Sing. This time, there were several safety nets in place. He would continue to see Dr. Holst intermittently and would attend group therapy on a daily basis. His family had chosen to play a more active role in his life, and Harold's overt resentment toward his mother had abated sufficiently for them to be able to live together in relative peace.

Harold was proactively seeking organizations and relationships that would strengthen the healing process. He would soon find a new residence at New York Theological Seminary, which provided a number of rooms for men in some form of recovery and rehabilitation. Concurrently, Harold was on a spiritual quest to find a "real faith." Was this, perhaps, the one component that had been missing on his journey toward healing?

HAROLD: I remember walking one night in the park and I met some women who had this table, and they were giving out free books, and one was *The Cross and the Switchblade* by Alex Cruz and David Wilkerson. I went home that night, and I read that book. I studied it for two days. It was really good, and I remember it gave me hope about the deliverance of God. It really gave me encouragement, and I thought to myself, "This guy is really living by faith. He's walking by faith. His whole life has been changed by faith." I wondered if I'd ever find a real faith like that.

I remember I used to pass a church on West Eleventh Street in the village, and I used to see a sign in psychedelic colors, and it said, "God Is Love." I used to stand in front of it, and I'd meditate on that sign— "God Is love"—and I'd find myself wondering if there really is a God of love.

DR. SAM: Harold left few stones unturned as he searched for that love and support that had been missing in his life. Though not a heavy or consistent drinker, he started attending AA meetings which were offered at the seminary where he was residing.

HAROLD: I heard this guy talk at AA one night. He told his story, and I heard honesty. I heard truth. I heard no lies. I heard no cover-ups. I heard fearlessness. I heard confidence. I heard the truths like those truths I was reading in the Bible in some way. His honesty impressed me. I remember saying I want what he has. I want it for me. I said in my heart, I want it for me. And somehow, I sensed that God would give it to me. Not then and there, but sometime...somewhere.

DR. SAM: In addition to AA, Harold attended group therapy sessions, a Hari Krishna retreat, joined the Fortune Society (dedicated to assisting ex-convicts), and even grew his hair long and hung out with the hippies in Washington Square Park who sang about Jesus and the angels, which, as Harold describes, "made me feel really good." And thanks to the radio given to him by his nephew Owen, he would listen to Family Radio at night and read his Bible.

Encouraged by the support groups he had surrounded himself with, Harold felt uplifted and nurtured and believed he was moving forward toward something, not knowing quite what that something was. Unexpectedly, a family tragedy would intervene.

HAROLD: At this time, my brother Steven opened up a store selling old clothes. My nephew Owen wanted to help open it—they were partners, I guess—and it wasn't open even a week when Owen got killed. Here's a kid that I loved so much. He was just a beautiful kid and had just turned twenty-one, and he was smoking grass and went downtown and bought some grass from a pusher, and it was bad stuff. And he went down to make a complaint and get his money back [not a smart thing to do], and they had an argument, and the dealer stabbed and shot and killed him.

I went to his funeral and just saw him lying there. It broke my heart. Here he is, this kid in a coffin, and my sister's all upset and the whole family is crying, and here he was, this sweet kid, in the coffin, dead. And it was like so many of my fears came back. Owen had to face what I feared for so many years—death—and it was like all these fears I'd had just came flooding back—fear of the Mafia, fear of not making it, fear of being made fun of, fear of being raped and castrated, and fear of cracking up all over again.

DR. SAM: Still seeking that "perfect love which casts out fear," Harold would revert to familiar patterns of behavior to assuage the fear and fill the void. Seeking intimacy, he continued to have casual sex with numerous partners and the consumption of food and more food became his drug de jour.

HAROLD: As you know, Dr. Sam, I was a compulsive eater to begin with. All I wanted to do was eat all the time when I was feeling insecure, unloved, and in pain. And then, they sent me to a new day center for more treatment where they put me on this medication that was making my metabolism go faster, or something like that, and I couldn't stop eating. It was like I was driven—I couldn't stop!

Every day I would go to the movies on Forty-Second Street where it was dark and I was alone and no one could see me, and I used to sit there all day and eat candy and cake and popcorn and drink sodas, one right after another. And then at night, when I went to bed, I was eating Häagen-Dazs ice cream! I couldn't stop, I just couldn't stop myself. I felt like this overstuffed sausage, and if I bent down, it felt like things were going to burst. I had problems breathing and could hardly walk. I mean, I was waddling when I was walking. I'd walk one or two blocks, and I'd have to sit and rest. When I walked up the stairs, I had to take one step at a time and I sounded like a locomotive, huffing and puffing away!

DR. SAM: Unable to control himself, Harold would soon weigh nearly three hundred pounds. He finally visited a medical doctor, and when the lab results came back, the doctor told him, in no uncertain terms, "You're going to die, Harold, if you don't lose weight." He had high blood pressure, high cholesterol, and was anemic and diabetic. Harold also knew that there was nothing he could do about it.

HAROLD: It was like a shock to me. I remember that whole week, I was like in this emotional turmoil, facing my death if I didn't lose the weight soon. And I knew in my heart that I couldn't lose weight, that I couldn't go on a diet and keep it off. I just knew it, Dr. Sam. I knew I was powerless over food and just couldn't manage my life.

DR. SAM: Like many other issues in his life, Harold was indeed powerless to help himself. Though necessary to the process, his healing would need more than proper medications; more than the valuable support groups he had joined; and more than all his good intentions, desire, and willpower to live a healthy and productive life.

Did Harold know that he had come at last to the end of his own resources? He speaks passionately into the tape recorder, keenly aware of his personal insufficiency.

HAROLD: I felt like I was trying to pull myself up by my bootstraps to get well—getting a job, getting the room at the seminary, doing all the things the doctors were telling me to do, teaching me to do, but it was all self-sufficiency. I can do it, I can handle it! But the truth is, Dr. Sam, I couldn't handle it. I was insufficient. I just couldn't go on anymore. I was so ugly and fat. I was so tired of struggling, of the daily fight, and I was so afraid that all the depression and fantasies and everything else would overtake me again, and I was trying to beat it in my own strength in some way, and I didn't know what else to do. But I knew there was something else—something else I needed, something else I'd been waiting for, and something else that I felt was coming.

DR. SAM: After another season of fear and self-hatred, was there about to be a turning point in Harold's torturous life? Would his prayers be answered? Was Harold about to open a door and allow the gift of God's healing to assist him in finding that "something else," that "real faith" he had been so earnestly seeking?

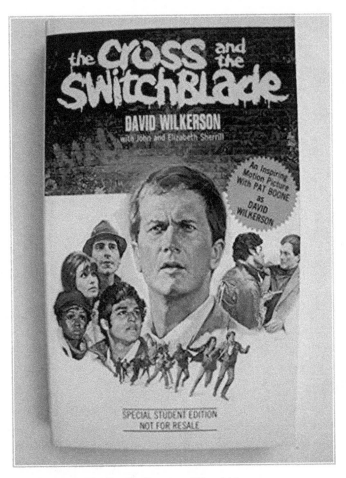

The book that gave Harold hope.

Chapter 13

God Help Me!

In the end, no one can avoid the cross.

DR. SAM: Harold had taken several simple steps toward his healing, but some days it seemed that for every step he took forward, he took two backward. Such is the path. The healing process wears no wristwatch or odometer. One must journey for a long time and a far way to find it. For sure, it is a marathon and not a sprint. But Harold had discovered a deep desire—"I wanted God to save my life"—and his steps were now being ordered in very specific ways.

HAROLD: One night I was just walking in the village and came across that sign again, the one in psychedelic colors that said "God Is Love." And all of a sudden, I saw some steps going down and a little sign on the steps—like cellar steps—you couldn't even see where it went, and it said, "Catacombs." And I walked down the steps and through a door and entered a beautiful room with burlap walls and tables with candles on them. I couldn't figure out what it was, but it was nice with soft music playing, and it was just so serene and quiet.

And there were these guys and ladies there who were dressed sort of like country or hippy—kind of like hippie and country combined—but they were Christians, real simple people and sweet, and introduced themselves to me and offered me ice-cold orange juice and cookies and stuff, and I really liked that, and there was this—I'll never forget this—record playing over and over again, "I've got the joy, joy, joy, joy down in my heart. Where? Down in my heart. Where? Down in my heart. I've got the joy, joy, joy, joy down in my heart. Down in my heart to stay!" And it was so nice to hear that theme and refrain again and again, and I really liked and appreciated it.

And there was this black brother there, and his name was Brother Timothy and he opened the Bible to me and started reading it to me. I just liked his calmness and his presence, and he took an interest in me, and I started coming night after night and started realizing I had another disease, Dr. Sam, and it was a disease in my heart. And I didn't have the Lord in my heart.

Dr. Sam: Harold had been drawn to that simple children's song that has been sung in nearly every vacation Bible school around the world. One of the verses says, "I've got the peace that passes understanding down in my heart." Another says, "I've got the love of Jesus, love of Jesus, down in my heart." Harold was longing for that peace and love.

Harold: I was hating myself again, Dr. Sam. I felt like that fat, unloved little boy whom the kids all made fun of. I felt like I knew Jesus was the truth, but I didn't have a hard faith. I didn't have a real faith. I wanted to give God my life, but I hadn't. I remembered that chorus we sang at the orphanage, "Jesus loves me this I know, for the Bible tells me so," and I wondered if it was possible for Jesus to love me…even me.

I remember late one night I left the seminary and went out walking, looking for something to eat. I had started a diet on my own—some crazy diet of very little food for three or four days—and my emotions were coming up. I was feeling, like, how am I gonna stop eating? I'm trying now, and I want to save my life, but I know I can't. And I still feel the fears and the paranoia, but I remember I was walking and didn't want to go back to my room and be alone, and I remember something in me prayed. And all of a sudden, it was if someone said, "Look up," and my head looked up, not of its own power, and I looked up and I saw this cross, and something in me yelled, "God, save me." It was a sincere prayer, and I said, "God, save me, I can't save myself." I meant it.

I came to the end of myself. I couldn't save myself, and I knew it, and I said, "Help me to stop overeating, and I'll give you my life. I'll give you my soul, Lord. Save me from the fear, from the Mafia, Lord, please save me. I've got nothing left, God. I'm a sinner. Save me!" I remember I talked to Him so sincere, and I felt like some part of me, something inside me, deep in my soul, shouted out involuntarily, "Help me, Jesus, and I'll live for you. God help me!"

DR. SAM: There's a verse in the Bible that says, "And everyone who calls on the name of the Lord will be saved" (Acts 2:21, NIV). That night, in rather dramatic fashion, Harold had called out to the Lord, and he *knew* that he had been saved.

HAROLD: And, Dr. Sam, I'm so glad I looked up at that cross. I couldn't escape the cross! Thank God! God was calling me, and I knew that He had heard my cry!

DR. SAM: It is only fitting that it would be beneath the cross that Harold would find the forgiveness, peace, and love he had been seeking. It reminds me of an old gospel hymn I used to sing in my youth: "Some through the fire, some through the flood, some through great sorrow, but all through the blood." Harold had gone through all of those stages, and now he was allowing the Great Physician—the greatest therapist of them all—to lead him forward on this journey of healing, a journey hand in hand! As it says in the Bible, "For I am the Lord your God who takes hold of your right hand and says to you, do not fear; I will help you" (Isa. 41:13, NIV).

Might this be the cross that Harold saw?

Chapter 14

An Uncommon Healing

To love that which you once hated is the greatest of miracles.

DR. SAM: There was nothing common about Harold. There was nothing common about his healing. His life's journey was uncommon (not too many of us hang around the Mafia!), and so would be his healing process. But a common denominator in all healing is letting go, and that evening, under the cross, Harold would let go and surrender all that he had been holding onto. The highs and lows of the road he had been on would begin to smooth out, and the healing would be fuller than anything he could have imagined on his own. He did know this: *The Lord was working, and things were moving very fast.*

HAROLD: It wasn't immediately right then and there. I think it was about, I don't know, two or three days later, or a week later, but somehow, I ended up in a Moravian church. I do remember some nice woman at an AA meeting had told me about this organization called Overeaters Anonymous. And somehow, I don't know how, but I must have heard that this Moravian Church had an OA meeting, and I went to this church and the meeting was in this crowded basement room—hardly an ideal place for a lot of big people and I could barely get in the doorway! And there was a speaker and he was speaking on how to cope with compulsive overeating, and it was just like Alcoholics Anonymous, except it was for overeaters, and I just knew right away that God had guided me there, and it was all very emotional. This guy came over to me after the meeting—Big Dakota, thank God for Big Dakota—and he told me how he had lost over a 150 lbs., and he reached out to me, hugged me, and gave me hope that I could too.

And I remember, Dr. Sam, I don't know if it was a week into the program or what, but I started looking at the steps. The first step was to believe in a power greater than me, and I knew that Jesus was my Higher Power and I had turned the will of my life into His care. And all of a sudden, the presence of God overcame me, and I knew immediately that with Christ as my Higher Power, OA fit in perfectly with Christianity and my faith.

DR. SAM: Harold still sought out official blessing for Overeaters Anonymous. In the sweet freshness of his newfound faith in Jesus, he was so concerned about OA and Christianity's compatibility that he went to an Episcopal priest (he was working at the parish as a custodian) and asked him, "Listen, I'm in OA, and their twelve steps, are they true? Or do they violate some of the Bible's teachings?" The good priest responded, "Harold, there's not one step in the program that violates God. It blesses Him and edifies Him. They're His principles." Harold was assured and told the priest, "Thank you, I'm home." And Harold took to his new home and his new faith as he had never taken to anything before.

HAROLD: When I walked into OA and they told their stories like I'm telling mine now and they shared their experiences, their hopes, their weaknesses, their pain, how they came to believe, what they were doing, how they were making it—it gave me strength, it gave me courage, and it gave me the faith that I could do it too. I saw the facts right in front of me, guys who couldn't sit and cross their legs, I saw them working on principles of faith from the Bible, and then they lost 50, a 100, a 150 lbs., and I identified with it completely!

I'm not saying that it was always easy because it's not, but I worked the tools of the program. Every morning I said, "First things first," got on my knees and admitted I was powerless over food, and admitted I couldn't manage my life and turned the will of my life over to Him and asked Him to fill me and direct me and teach me and guide me and bless me. I said, "Lord, keep me safe through this one day. Just for today, help me to make the phone calls. Call my sponsor. Help me go to the meetings. Guide me where I should go. Give me the strength and the daily bread I need only for today!" And He blessed me, Dr. Sam, oh how He blessed me!

DR. SAM: Harold interrupts his reminiscences, and rather than address me on the tape recorder, he starts thanking God in a litany of praise for the many blessings that have flowed into his life.

HAROLD: Lord Jesus, I just want to stop right now to thank You, thank You for your presence. Thank You that I know I'm saved, that my sins have been washed away by your precious blood. Thank You for helping me stop eating too much 'cause You know I can't save my own life. Thank You for OA and for my wonderful sponsor. Thank You for taking away my fear of the Mafia, Lord, and for protecting me even when I didn't know You. Thank You for taking away my guilt and those chains I felt like I was all wrapped up in. Thank You that I'm home, that Your presence has taken over my soul. Thank You, Jesus, that I'm free! I'm free! You rescued me! You gave me such a present, dear Jesus, and I just want to thank You now! Oh, and, Lord Jesus, I almost forgot—thank You for my doctors! They really cared for me even though I didn't understand some of them. I thank You, Jesus, for them and for sending so many kind and wonderful people into my life!

DR. SAM: Wow! Imagine this psychologist's delight over Harold's reverie of praise. I found myself thanking God for the deep work of healing He was doing in Harold's life. Personally, I was grateful that this experimental exercise of recalling and recording Harold's life experiences was proving to be more than a simple catharsis. In a very real sense, Harold was participating in the ongoing process of his healing. His prayers for forgiveness and the blessing of his abusers is in stark contrast to his previous resentments.

HAROLD: Lord, you're the God of all eternity, and maybe when Miss B died, you knew then what I was going to ask you today. So even then, you could have touched her and said, "Forgive Harold," and maybe she forgave me, and maybe she forgave herself. So forgive all the sins she ever did to me, Lord, conscious or unconscious, willingly or unwillingly. Forgive her and bless her, Lord, and forgive me for my attitude of revenge and anger and hatred toward her. I ask you now, by the Holy Spirit, to just touch that anger and resentment—that surliness that I used to give to Miss Banderhoff. I hope to see her in heaven, Lord. Bless her, Father. In Jesus's name, amen.

DR. SAM: Reflected in Harold's prayer are *both* his request for personal forgiveness and for the forgiveness of his abusers. Harold had reached a point of deep understanding which led him to a profound forgiveness. As I listened to his prayer of blessing for Miss B, I couldn't help but be reminded of the apostle Paul who was blinded when encountering the living Christ on the road to Damascus, only later for the scales to fall from his eyes, resulting in Paul seeing the world in a radically different way. As the scales of resentment and hatred fell from Harold's eyes, he went from the abused child and abusive man to seeing life in a radically new way. He describes his own new birth in near mystical terms: "It was like a whole new universe came into me and it was an awesome experience." Harold had been given new eyes in which to see the world.

HAROLD: I didn't hate Maria. I didn't hate the Mafia. I still had some anxieties, but they went away. I still had some fears, but they went away. His loving presence was in me, and it was all around me, and it uplifted and guided me. It was as if, Dr. Sam, I saw everybody with new eyes. I just have to praise God! And may I never, never hurt anybody again, dear Lord. And may I never be hurt again, dear Lord, and bless those who did those things to me, Lord Jesus, bless them and me with your beautiful forgiveness, in Jesus's name.

DR. SAM: It is rare to witness such a transformation, and it confirms the truth of the Good News: "Therefore, if anyone is in Christ, the new creation has come: The old has gone, the new is here!" (2 Cor. 5:17, NIV).

Of course, there were no quick-and-easy fixes here. This was a journey of uncommon healing filled with breakthroughs and relapses time and again. Harold could have easily fallen between the cracks—the abandoned boy and forgotten man—but with the help of God and His caretakers along the way, he went from the forgotten man to the restored man. And in this one thing, Harold was now confident: "The Lord is my strength and my song, he has given me victory. This is my God and I will praise him" (Exod. 15:2, NIV).

The OA meeting room in the Moravian Church continues.

Chapter 15

A Transformed Life

God never changes—his children do.

DR. SAM: If I were inclined to cynicism (which I am not!), I might find Harold's story Pollyannaish, with an inevitable happy ending. His story has nothing to do with happiness. In order to survive, Harold needed a deep peace in his life, a peace more satisfying than the many substitutes he had indulged in while seeking happiness. It was difficult work, and he had to lean on the power of the Spirit each step of the way.

HAROLD: I kept going to meetings three times a day, making phone calls, and helping other people as best as I could. It wasn't easy, that's for sure. I was calling people every time I had a desire to eat. I would walk down the street and I'd look at food, and a little voice would say *no* and, like, an invisible force would just turn my head away. I'd just say, "Thank you, Lord." I'd look at a woman with wrong sexual feelings, and I'd just hear that little voice say *no*, and my head would automatically turn. And I'd just say, "Thank you, Jesus," and this sense of peace would come over me.

DR. SAM: Harold's commitment to God, the program of Overeaters Anonymous, daily group therapy, and Bible study, along with consistent church attendance, would all combine to make the radical difference in Harold's perception of himself and the world. These elements working in tandem gave Harold an emotional equilibrium he had never experienced before. Even his family couldn't help but take notice.

HAROLD: Everybody saw a change in me, a transformation. Where there had been so much hatred, they saw love in me now. My whole family could see it. I would go over to my mother's house, and she'd say, "I can see a change in your eyes, Harold." And I'd tell her about Jesus and told her it was like I had been born again, and my brothers, well, they looked at me like I was kind of strange. They'd do double takes, and I'd just keep talking about Jesus and how he saved me, and they saw me losing the weight. I lost about a hundred pounds in a little less than five months. It all was a little too much for them, my brothers. One time, they said, "We wish you were like you were before." But I wasn't going back. No way! And gradually they accepted me as this changed person.

Father, I ask you right now, Jesus, keep me from ever going back to the old life. I believe you will! Thank you, Lord.

DR. SAM: Even without his family's understanding and full support, there would be no turning back for Harold this time. His validation would come from within and from drawing on the "means of grace" made available to him.

HAROLD: I couldn't stop reading the Bible. No matter where I went, it was like a force. It was like a map. I carried it with me all the time and just couldn't stop reading it. And I started going to church on Sundays and Wednesday nights...it was like I wanted to be in God's house all the time. And I kept going to my meetings at that little Moravian Church.

One night, this small, young woman gave her story, and it was like she was talking about me. She talked about living all alone in this tiny room with only a bed, dresser, and chair. She talked about her fears and the paranoia. It was not the Mafia, of course, but it was the same kind of fears—the same seclusion, the overeating, the running from God, and I was, like, transfixed listening to her and I saw myself in her and thought, "That's me. That's me."

There was a big sign that was above her—the serenity prayer—and there were those two words in there, "I can." And as she was speaking, I looked at those words, "I can," and inside me, there was a click. It was like a turn. I don't know if it was a conscious decision or what, but it was like something inside of my whole being turned from negative to positive, and it said, "I can too. With God's help, I can too!" God bless that woman wherever she is now.

DR. SAM: With each passing day, Harold was gaining strength and confidence in his ability to live a healthy and productive life. He was now free to experience positive intimacy in his personal relationships.

HAROLD: I met this fellow in the OA program, and I used to wonder if he was a hit man or something. Okay, I admit it, I guess I was still a little suspicious with people I didn't know. Anyway, he drove me home one day and asked me about myself, and I told him...told him everything, the truth about myself. And as I was about to get out of the car, he started telling me about himself. He was a dentist, and when he graduated from school, he didn't go into dentistry here but gave two years of his life to some kind of a Catholic outreach in Africa, and he got his friends to contribute all the dental equipment and served there for two years, and that really impressed me.

Then he tells me that later on, when he had his own big dentist office back in the States, he absconded—I think that's the word he used—funds from Medicaid and was sent to prison. Wow, I thought, this was quite a story. And as I was stepping out of the car, my Bible fell out on the floor of the car, and he picked it up and gave it back to me and later told me he always took that as a sign that there was a special bond between us. And that's how it began.

He was having trouble with food, and as I got to know him over the next few weeks, he asked me if I would be his sponsor, and I said yes. Later, we sat down and had coffee, and I went over the steps with him—just like my sponsor, Drake, did—and I shared my experiences with him, my strengths and hopes, and we became very, very good friends and have had a friendship one day at a time ever since. We understand each other. He's an ex-con, I'm an ex-con. His father committed suicide, my father committed suicide. He's an overeater, I'm an overeater—or, rather, we're both recovering overeaters. God put us in each other's life. I have to say, he's my best friend. We've called one another now on a daily basis for the past six and a half years.

DR. SAM: When this journey of uncommon healing began, it was difficult to imagine that such a healthy, long-term relationship like this one could ever exist for Harold. But gone were the muggings, the stickups, the Mafia, the hatred, the abuse of others, the shame, the self-loathing, the destructive behavior. Harold was now ready to publicly announce and affirm his newfound faith in Christ.

HAROLD: I was reading a lot about baptism. I said, "Lord, show me when to get baptized, how to get baptized, what it's for. Teach me, 'cause I don't understand it," and the Lord led me to eight months of repenting—of dying like that old caterpillar was dying and becoming a butterfly—eight months 'til I went to Calvary Baptist Church up on Fifty-Seventh Street, where I asked the pastor, "Pastor, I want full acceptance and blessing of God in my life. I am not the old Harold anymore. I'm a new man. Would you baptize me?" And, praise God, the pastor said, "Yes, I will," and I was baptized!

DR. SAM: Below is a record of Harold's baptism, found in the archives of Calvary Baptist Church, New York City, New York.

> Baptismal Candidates
> Baptized by Rev. Nelson Schoen
> September 21, 1975
> Mr. Harold Johnson: Unemployed, Messenger
> Requested Scripture: "I am crucified with Christ: nevertheless I live; yet not I, but Christ liveth in me: and the life which I now live in the flesh I live by the faith of the Son of God, who loved me, and gave himself for me" (Gal. 2:20, King James Version).
> Requested Hymn: "Turn Your Eyes Upon Jesus"

Dr. Sam: With that single act of baptism, Harold was renouncing his old way of living and saying, "I will, with God's help," to his new life in Jesus Christ. May you and I join Harold in praying this baptismal prayer for ourselves: "Oh, Lord, send us into the world in witness to your love. Teach us to love others in the power of the Spirit!" Harold was now ready to go into the world and bear witness to God's love!

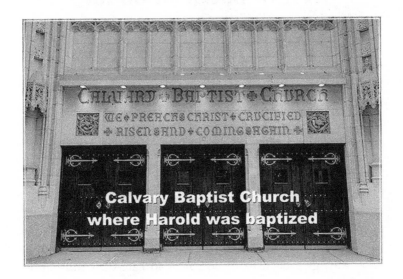

Calvary Baptist Church where Harold was baptized

Chapter 16

A New Badge of Honor

Giving is the path to freedom.

DR. SAM: The year following his baptism, Harold moved into the Lamb's and began attending church there, under the leadership of the Reverend Paul Moore. He was surrounded by a loving pastor and "brothers and sisters in Christ" who encouraged him in his faith. He continued to counsel with Dr. Holst and shared with him what God had been doing in his life. They both agreed that it was time for Harold to reach out to others and, in some way, give back to those who had cared for him along the way.

HAROLD: Dr. Holst was telling me to do something constructive, "Get out of yourself, Harold, and serve somebody." Of all places, he suggested that I consider volunteering at Bellevue Hospital! So what happened is, I cautiously went back to Bellevue and submitted an application for a volunteer position, and much to my surprise, they accepted me! Turns out, it was really nice to be back on those wards because this time, I was led by the Spirit and not by my selfish self.

I had a New Testament in in my pocket, and I'd visit the patients one on one, and I started to get to know them. I'd serve them water and bring them magazines and newspapers, and I'd sit and talk and listen and hold their hands, and if they wanted me to read the Bible, I'd read the Bible and pray with them. It was just so wonderful. And much of the time we didn't even talk about the Lord. I would just sit and listen and be kind and friendly to them.

DR. SAM: Bellevue Hospital was a place that Harold knew all too well. Some of his memories of it were horrific: He had bit off a portion of his lower lip while there and at one point had covered his body with his own excrement. It was a place where he had been handcuffed to a bed, and now he was going from bed to bed and, like that nurse who patted him on the back and told him it would be okay, was sharing his own words of kindness to those who were in physical and emotional pain.

HAROLD: A neighbor, one of my mother's dear friends that lived in our building, got very sick and had cancer. I used to go visit her when I was there, and she ended up dying later. But many times when I would visit her, she would give me a big smile and thank me. I remember I used to bring her ice cream, and little cakes—but I wouldn't eat any myself!—and she would thank me over and over. She was just so thankful that I came to visit her.

I remember another time there was a guy on the ward with lots of problems, and it turns out it was a guy from my old neighborhood. I knew him when I was in my twenties, when I was banging guys out left and right. He was a real tough guy, like I once was, and we started talking, and he said, "Gee, what are you doing here in the hospital, Harold?" I said, "Well, I'm doing volunteer work. I got away from the old neighborhood and God's changed my life." He thought that was nice and said to me, "That's good, Harold. That's good." He was really appreciative when I'd come and visit him, and I really felt good being around him and all the other sick people there. It was like I was doing something rewarding and worthwhile.

DR. SAM: After some essential training, Harold was designated an official volunteer and given a brown Bellevue Hospital volunteer jacket. He wore that jacket with great pride. He was no longer the ridiculed child whom Miss Banderhoff had capriciously named Riley. He was no longer the orphan kid called "Baldy," taunted for his shaved head. He was now an officially recognized volunteer; and his full moniker, Harold Johnson, was on his name badge to prove it! And that name badge, not a bald head, would be his new badge of honor—a symbol of acceptance, trust, and validity.

Nothing would give Harold greater pride and pleasure than to wear that name badge pinned to his volunteer jacket as he walked those hospital halls caring for the needs of others.

HAROLD: Working at Bellevue made me feel so good. I used to do it every Sunday afternoon and once during the week when I wasn't working as a messenger. People just couldn't wait 'til I would come by! I'd walk down the hall, and they'd say, "Hi, Harold!" and I'd bring gifts to them when I could afford them. Then I started to go to intensive care units to the people who were critical and on the machines, and I would pray for them, and I would stand by their beds and hold their hands, and I would watch those heart machines go "beep, beep, beep," and I was so glad that God had put me there...

next to them and their heartbeats. I just loved being there, praying and holding their hands.

I just have to stop, Dr. Sam, and say, "Thank you, Jesus. I had prayed to you, Lord Jesus, to help me have compassion on others that are sick, and you answered that prayer!"

DR. SAM: More than anything else, Harold's care for others at Bellevue Hospital was dramatic evidence of his healing. As I listened to Harold's thank-you to Jesus, even this subdued counselor had to say with the apostle Paul: "Praise be to the God and Father of our Lord Jesus Christ, the Father of compassion and the God of all comfort, who comforts us in all our troubles, so that we can comfort those in any trouble with the comfort we ourselves receive from God" (2 Cor. 1:3–4, NIV). Others would now be the beneficiary of the healing and comfort Harold had received, and Harold was full of thanks and praise to the One from whom he had received it.

HAROLD: Oh, Lord, you know how sick I was, but it's all under the blood by the power of the Holy Spirit. Thank you, Jesus. I thank you that I've gotten all this out on the tape recorder for Dr. Sam and for You, dear Lord. I thank you for washing it all away. I know by your death and resurrection, Lord, it is finished. My fear is finished. I thank you, God. I thank you, Jesus. Glory to you, Lord. The victory is won. I thank you for just replacing everything with your love, with your Word, with health, with wholeness. I'm healed—I know that. Thank you, Lord. Thank you, Jesus.

DR. SAM: From a life of abandonment, abuse, abusiveness, and mental illness, Harold had been helped by many caring individuals, culminating in his repentant cry of

"God help me!" Now, it would be family, friends, and patients at the hospital who would be receiving *his* caring acceptance and love.

Harold's story had come full circle and can only be explained as an extraordinary journey of redemption and restoration—a journey of uncommon healing.

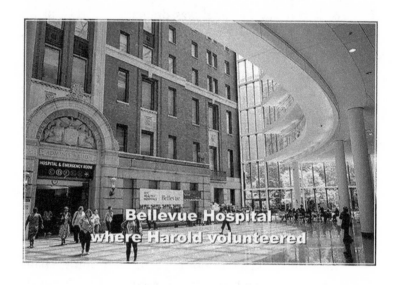

Epilogue

No Mourners

DR. SAM: Harold exited this world as he had entered it—quietly. Records have not been found confirming when he was born, which was probably sometime in the early 1930s. According to the Reverend Orville Jenkins, pastor of the Lamb's Manhattan Church of the Nazarene at the time, Harold died sometime in late 1985 or early 1986.

Years earlier, as a young boy at the orphanage, one of the few joyful days Harold experienced was when Miss Banderhoff had called on him to carry the candlelit cake celebrating Jesus's birthday. But from the moment when Harold looked up at the cross and cried out "God help me," he was celebrating his "new birth" day in Christ every day of the year! This new life is what friends and acquaintances remember about Harold. There are no mourners but, rather, celebrants who rejoice with Harold over the healing power of God's love.

Below are a few remembrances from individuals who knew Harold and witnessed the joy of his transformed life.

The Reverend Paul Moore, Pastor Emeritus, Lamb's Ministries: "As the founding pastor of the Lamb's Church in the midseventies, our Sunday worship services were characterized by joyful singing and an occasional 'Amen' or even 'Preach it, brother' during the sermon. But it was Harold, when hearing a message on the unconditional love of God, who would spontaneously break into laughter. It was not a guarded chuckle for this orphaned but redeemed child of God—no, it was a deep-down belly laugh exploding in gratitude for his salvation. With Harold's 'cup running over,' the more sophisticated and well-behaved parishioner sitting nearby was reminded of this liberating truth: Lost persons found, snatched from the hold of Satan, and welcomed into the Body of Christ have every reason for holy laughter. Often, in midsermon, I'd pause when I heard Harold's signature laughter and give him space to joyfully laugh in praise for being a part of the family of God!"

Jim and Dustee Hullinger, Harold's friends and colaborers in ministry at the Lamb's Church: "Some of our ladies called him *sweet*; younger folks called him *gentle*; we all called him *tender*. Our friend, Harold, was a loving presence in our lives. His ready smile and easygoing nature belied the hurt and torment that had plagued him in years past. That seemed to make his calm demeanor all the more meaningful. Often, just passing him in the hallway with a warm hello would give rise to Harold's unique laugh, which was his way of affirming you. Harold made our community richer as we found ourselves amazed at his extraordinary testimony of God's love and grace."

Effie, staff pianist at the Lamb's Church: "Harold reminded me of that odd relative whom you were a little nervous about meeting again—never knowing quite what to expect—only to be delighted when you did meet again. That was Harold. You knew he'd been to hell and back and that it was God who had rescued him. And so you found yourself taken back a bit, really humbled, because you were in the presence of one of God's miracles. Harold and I had the same dentist who thought Harold was just the greatest guy in the world. And so he was—Praise God!"

Dr. Michael Christensen, former associate pastor, Lamb's Church: "Beyond his holy laugh in worship, in which we all took delight, I remember with fondness Harold's simple faith, spiritual innocence, gentle presence, and holy life. He reminded me, as a Yale Divinity School student at the time, that real Christianity was not found in books or complex theology—it was found in someone like Harold. God rest his dear soul."

Judi Cochran Reynolds, music director at the Lamb's Church, recording artist: "I remember sitting on the steps of the Lamb's with Harold, and we'd talk about dieting. He wanted to help me because he knew I wanted to lose weight and, like himself, suffered somewhat with my self-image. He'd lost all this weight and was as trim and fit as could be. He was really kind and gentle as he shared with me his own challenges Then we'd talk about the Lord, and in many ways, Harold was like a little, harmless, precious boy. We were different but equals in Christ, and I was able to have these very human conversations with him. I didn't feel like I was ministering but, rather, sharing with a trusted friend. We'd share scripture and would laugh and cry over what the Lord had done for both of us. Harold's gratitude was infectious. What a privilege to call him a friend!"

Rev. Orville Jenkins Jr., former pastor of the Lamb's Church, officiant at Harold's funeral: "I conducted Harold's funeral not long after we helped him move out of the Lamb's building and into his own apartment. Harold was an extraordinary, unique individual with a vibrant public persona. Over the years, he had become a fixture at the Lamb's and was greatly missed after he passed. I was honored to be his pastor."

Bill Brehm, staff photographer at the Lamb's: "Harold Johnson was a good friend and brother to me during my years working and living at the Lamb's (1976–1981). I especially remember an act of kindness he did for me on day. I was short of money—and food—because of circumstances beyond my control. Realizing my problem, Harold gave me lunch, an act for which I was so grateful."

D. Paul Thomas, actor and playwright at the Lamb's: "He was a force of nature. We collided once in the stairwell of the Lamb's, Harold nearly knocking me over as he bounded up the old marble steps two at a time. He laughed his characteristic laugh and apologized profusely. I told him, 'It's okay, it's okay, I wasn't watching where I was going, Harold!'

"At the time, I had no idea of his challenging background and always thought of him as this very sweet guy. But one look into Harold's eyes and you knew he had travelled a very difficult road. He would tell me how he really enjoyed the theater and encourage me in my playwriting. Truth is, Harold came up to 'the bat of life' with two strikes against him. He had a very mercurial, sensitive nature, with tremendous energy. Under different circumstances, Harold might have found his calling as an actor, a poet, a pastor, perhaps a gourmet chef. As it turned out, he became the most important thing—a follower of Christ."

EPILOGUE

Afterward

While working on Harold's story, I also have been the night-time caregiver for my dear wife, Arlene. She and I have been married sixty-one years, having been sweethearts since meeting at Olivet Nazarene University in 1956.

Precious Arlene is now in the final stage of Lewy body dementia, a neurodegenerative disease, and the same disease that took the life of Glen Campbell and struck Robin Williams, who chose to end his life prior to losing his faculties from this debilitating disease.

Arlene's illness began over seven years ago. Her symptoms included severe memory loss, some Parkinson's activity, visual hallucinations, paranoid thoughts, fear, anxiety, and hostility. Along the way, she lost most of her vision from shingles concentrated in one eye and macular degeneration in the other eye.

Prior to the disease, Arlene had been an active and loving wife, mother, and grandmother. She was a great cook and hostess and a huge support to me as I traveled many miles during my work life. She was involved in Bible study groups and helped develop the first women's ministry at First Church of the Nazarene, Pasadena, California.

As I worked on Harold's story, I couldn't help but reflect on the contrasting parallels with Arlene's story. Harold had gone from severe darkness into the light. Arlene was going from the light to severe mental and physical darkness. Harold had gone from confusion to clarity. Arlene's journey was from clarity to constant confusion. Harold's fears had slowly abated. Arlene's fears were increasing. But throughout both opposing processes, grace has abounded, thanks to Arlene and Harold's connection to the ultimate Light of this world.

Arlene's connection to the Light has been in her new-found ability to spontaneously sing the Christian hymns and choruses of her youth. As can be the case in dementia patients, melodies and their accompanying words may be vividly recalled while little else is remembered. In Arlene's case, I and the family were amazed because she was neither an energetic nor tuneful singer in the past, only reluctantly and quietly joining in when songs were sung during the worship service. Now, Arlene sings the verses and choruses of her favorite songs in near perfect pitch and with deep emotion. We're grateful this gift of song has been given to her, as she enjoys singing her favorites throughout the day. But like Harold's story, Arlene's journey has been a long and arduous one.

Initial indications of the disease were a series of Parkinson reactions, including severe muscle jerks and night terrors. This was followed by memory loss. She was soon evaluated, and early treatment was started with a brilliant research neurologist, Dr. Shankle. A spinal fluid assessment indicated extremely high and abnormal substances that damage the brain and impair the processing of information. It was then that the diagnosis of Lewy body dementia was confirmed. Intravenous medications, oral medications, and a potent medication in a skin patch form were all employed to control the disease, as there is no cure for it as of yet. All of this treatment was being done at home, and even though her symptoms improved somewhat, the immune boost medications had to be moved from the IV to a nasal infusion (the veins could no longer support the intravenous activity), and a severe irritation by the adhesive of the skin patch required its termination. But even in the midst of these setbacks, grace abounded.

Two caring and supportive pharmacists who operate a small local pharmacy took an interest in Arlene's treatment and found a way to get the patch-based medication compounded into a dispenser that allowed direct placement on the skin and with no irritation! Praise God! That process is now being used by several dementia patients in the area.

But even with the best medical and pharmaceutical support, Arlene continued to have frightening visual hallucinations; rapid, uncontrolled hand and arm movements; delusions that someone or something would harm or kill her (not unlike Harold's delusions); and times of aspirations due to her throat muscles not working properly. And like Harold, who admitted to himself that he was sick and helpless to do anything about it, my precious Arlene, even in the midst of her confusion, has had times of awareness, saying, "I can't do anything. I am going to die. Please, let me die."

I knew the reality of this disease when Arlene's primary physician told me that she probably had twelve to eighteen months to live. In the face of that, I prayed often and fervently for a God-given miracle, common *or* uncommon would be fine by me. (Although none of God's miracles are "common!") Many of those petitions for healing were at night—sometimes when she was able to sleep, other times during the unrest of her confusion and pronounced anxiety. But grace continued to abound; and during the third year after Arlene's initial diagnosis, she had fewer, less intense, emotional disturbances and hallucinations. She was now able to sit with the family after dinner and watch television without the chaotic reactions she'd previously experienced. For that, I have to say, "Thanks be to God!" I'd forgotten how relaxing an hour of TV can be!

Then at a regular scheduled visit, Dr. Shankle asked if I would consider Arlene having another spinal assessment done, since she was already outliving the normal life expectancy for this supposed final stage of the disease. I was concerned that her physical and mental condition might make the spinal tap difficult, even dangerous. But with his encouragement, I agreed to the procedure, and arrangements were made with the hospital.

Much like the caring nurse at Bellevue who told Harold that everything was going to be okay, as Arlene was being admitted to the pre-op area, another caring person (a dear physician friend) arrived and literally took charge in preparing her (even pushing the gurney to the radiology department), helping her onto the table, and taking her back to the discharge area when the procedure was completed. All the while, I was tagging along and watching the surprised looks of nurses and staff to see a senior physician serving a patient in this manner. Grace was abounding as this wonderful doctor told me and Arlene that everything was going to be okay.

Several weeks later, I drove Arlene to Hoag Hospital (along with her trusty wheelchair) to see Dr. Shankle and obtain the spinal test results. When we entered his office, he was standing beside a large computer screen and staring intently at us. It was strange for him to greet us in such an intense manner. His first words to me and Arlene were, "It's a miracle!" I was not accustomed to hearing the word *miracle* from medical personnel, and I had no idea why he was saying that. The good doctor then swung the screen around and showed me the results from the spinal fluid test done three years earlier versus the most recent test results.

In simple terms, two types of bad materials (proteins) were identified in both tests. Both were extremely high and abnormal in the first test. One type remained extremely high and abnormal in the most recent test. The second type had dropped to a normal level. The doctor explained that this second type, when found in the spinal fluid, is expected to increase 10 percent each year until death. Arlene's test had dropped to normal, the basis for what Dr. Shankle called a miracle.

Arlene didn't leave the office that day a fully restored person, but something miraculous had transpired. Praise God! And even though Arlene's life had been extended, I continued to pray for her complete healing. But one evening while praying, I sensed God's message to me was, *This is how I am healing her.* I realized then that my dear Arlene's healing (like that of Harold's) would be an uncommon one.

To this day, Arlene remains at home with wonderful and caring daytime assistance, aided by my nighttime assistance. In the process, her caregivers have learned some great Christian music, and several share with Arlene a relationship with Jesus. A chorus from Arlene's early church days is one of her favorites: "Did anybody tell you I love you today? Let me be the first, put me on your list—I love you and God loves you, and that's how it should be!" What peace fills the room when Arlene and friends and caregivers sing that song together. Like Harold, there is no greater peace than the peace that comes from knowing that God loves YOU! That song and other choruses, like "I'll say yes, Lord, yes, to your will and to your way," continue to lift my and Arlene's spirits, and were written by a dear friend of ours, Lynn Keesecker. When Lynn wrote these songs, little did he realize the enormous comfort his music would provide Arlene from the discomfort of this bewildering, mind-bending disease.

Recently, while I was giving Arlene her morning infusion treatment, she began humming the tune to an old song, "Farther along we'll know all about it. Farther along we'll understand why." I know she has always believed that, and even with the mental limitations of dementia, she still knows it and believes it!

Like Arlene, I too believe it—*We'll understand it better by and by*—but I continue also to believe this: "Therefore I tell you, whatever you ask for in prayer, believe that you have received it, and it will be yours"(Mark 11:24, NIV). Now, sometimes the healing we pray for and the healing that subsequently comes, comes to us in different ways than anticipated. Sometimes it comes to us through persons who are believers or, if not believers, through persons behaving in ways patterned by Christ. Sometimes it comes to us instantaneously, and other times it comes progressively. And as with Arlene and Harold, sometimes the healing comes out of a long and circuitous journey. For certain, healing comes to us in our "earthen vessels" and functions within our mental, physical, and spiritual conditions.

But through it all—whatever the specific nature of the healing—God's mercy, forgiveness, and unconditional love infuse our lives and those around us, offering us healing in distinct ways, all given to us by a good and caring God. As Harold would say, "*I just want to pause now and say, Thank You, Jesus!*"

Dr. Sam Mayhugh
Newport Beach, California
June 2019

New Lambs Sign

An Invitation

I wrote this book to bring hope to persons who have experienced abandonment, abuse (physical, emotional, or sexual), personal loss, dangerous behaviors, and, not the least, acute psychiatric events in their lives. You may not identify with this whole cluster of disturbing conditions, but all of us live imperfectly in an imperfect world and are subject to the pain and destructiveness of various issues and circumstances, whether driven from within or without—usually both.

More than anything, Harold and I wanted this "journey of uncommon healing" to bring vivid evidence to the power of God's redemption and restoration and to the power He gives to all of his wounded healers for ministering to others—with or without emblazoned jackets and name badges!

If, as you read this, you are personally in need of support, course adjustment, forgiveness, and unconditional love, would you please consider the cross and Harold's simple request—"God, help me!"—and take advantage of those persons and programs that are signposts for a healing and healthy journey.

To help you on your way, TBN has a prayer partner line available to you 24/7 at 888-73-1000 (in the United States) or 1-714-731-1000 (international).

Yours in Christ,
Dr. Sam

Dr. Sam presenting Lamb's counseling
center in NYC—1978.

About the Author

Samuel Mayhugh, PhD, is an executive psychologist who recently retired from IBH, a behavioral healthcare company he founded thirty-one years ago. His professional life has also been spent in private practice, treating patients in hospitals and outpatient offices, including the Lamb's Ministries in New York City.

He graduated from Olivet Nazarene University, Purdue University, and Indiana State University. He attended postgraduate certificate programs at Harvard and Oxford University.

For seven years he served as Chief Clinical Services at the renowned Las Encinas Hospital in Pasadena, California. More recently, Dr. Sam was Special Contractor for the US Department of Homeland Security. He also served on the Board of Directors of Victory Films, a Hollywood-based movie company producing "films of inspiration."

Dr. Sam has authored five works, including *C.I.P. Counseling Interaction Profile* (Association for Productive Teaching, 1969) and a coauthored text, *Managed Behavioral Health Care; an Industry Perspective*, with Sharon A. Shueman, PhD, and Warwick G. Troy, PhD, MPH, (Charles C. Thomas, Springfield, Illinois, 1994).

Beyond his duties as an executive psychologist and president of IBH, Dr. Sam has assisted church leaders and directors throughout the United States, supporting missionaries and indigenous church leaders in Central and South America and Africa.

In addition to sailing and an occasional spin around the formula car racetrack, one of the great joys of Dr. Sam's life has been in opening up his home to many weary sojourners who have found rest and restoration there, thanks to his wise counsel and the loving encouragement of his wife, Arlene.

CPSIA information can be obtained
at www.ICGtesting.com
Printed in the USA
FSHW012132201219